Growing a Beloved Community

Growing a Beloved Community

Twelve Hallmarks of a Healthy Congregation

Tom Owen-Towle

SKINNER HOUSE BOOKS
BOSTON

Copyright © 2004 by Tom Owen-Towle. Published by Skinner House Books. Skinner House Books is an imprint of the Unitarian Universalist Association, a liberal religious organization with more than 1,000 congregations in the U.S. and Canada. 25 Beacon St., Boston, MA 02108-2800.

Cover design by Kathryn Sky-Peck.
Text design by Suzanne Morgan.
Printed in United States

09 08 07 06 05
10 9 8 7 6 5 4 3 2

The poem on page 73 by Rudy Nemser is reprinted by permission of his daughter, Tobey Nemser.

ISBN 1-55896-464-9

Library of Congress Cataloging-in-Publication Data

Owen-Towle, Tom.
    Growing a beloved community : twelve hallmarks of a healthy congregation / Tom Owen-Towle.
        p. com.
    ISBN 1-55896-464-9 (alk. paper)
    1. Unitarian Universalist churches—Membership. 2. Church growth—Unitarian Universalists. 3. Evangelistic work. I. Title.

BX9842.O94 2004
289.1'32—dc22   2003070405

To the members and friends of First Unitarian Universalist Church of San Diego, who for twenty-four years respectfully and affectionately companioned its co-ministers, my wife Carolyn and me, as we grew a portion of the Beloved Community where we were planted.

—Tom Owen-Towle

Contents

Introduction

Blessed are you who know that the work of the church is transformation of society, who have a vision of Beloved Community transcending the present, and who do not shrink from controversy, sacrifice, or change. Blessed are you indeed.

—John Buehrens

BECAUSE OF UNITARIAN UNIVERSALISM's radical commitment to the personal search for truth and meaning, we sometimes forget that it is much more than an essentially individualistic religion. Our faith, at its fullest, is composed of confessions, matured into covenants and incarnated in communities. The Unitarian Universalist path is more a communal spiritual journey than a personal exploration of faith.

Theology, important as it is, is only a portion of the larger field of ecclesiology, which studies the nature and function of church. Ecclesiology raises important questions about with whom and how to practice a maturing faith. It maintains that the growth of a soul is the work not of an individual but of a community. It charges our independent wills to serve the interdependent web. Unitarian Universalist theologian James Luther Adams goes to the heart of the matter: "If a theological or ethical commitment does not issue in associational preference or transformation, it is to this extent not yet clear or meaningful. By their groups, their associational fruits, shall ye know them."

Rather than focus upon the all-too-familiar dumb and destructive things our parishes do, I've chosen to accentuate the positive, encourage the possibilities, spur us on toward the very best we can become. Consequently, I've pinpointed twelve hallmarks of healthy, vital Unitarian Universalist congregational life.

Churches will be obliged to make their own additions and corrections to my list. Rarely will any one congregation exhibit growth in all areas. But in parish, as in personal life, Unitarian Universalists live more by our aspirations than by our accomplishments. This book offers both theological grounding and practical guideposts for growing a Beloved Community and for measuring the strength and relevance of a congregation.

Growing a Beloved Community is for Sunday worshipers, board leaders, parish ministers, social action devotees, and religious educators—all of whom bravely build bridges of hope between pulpit and pew and the larger universe. It simply shares notes on how to do and be church the Unitarian Universalist way.

My earliest, formative glimpse of the Beloved Community was as a theological school student in 1965, when Dr. Martin Luther King Jr. summoned people of faith to Selma, Alabama, to raise a righteous ruckus. I'd never been in the South before. Our sole job as seminary students, every day, was to clear the fields of cow dung and then to set up huge tents for the civil rights marchers. In the evenings, we enjoyed the incredible talents of Dick Gregory; Peter, Paul and Mary; and other activist entertainers. I'll never forget Andy Young—later congressman, U.S. representative to the United Nations, and governor of Georgia, but then one of King's young lieutenants—shouting, "Hey, we're here to love the hell out of Alabama!" A bold Universalist decree, if there ever was one.

Remember, the nonviolence of Martin Luther King Jr. was tough-minded and strong-hearted. It resisted wrongdoing and challenged sloth. King's mission was clear. As he said after the

Montgomery bus boycott, "The end is reconciliation; the end is redemption, the end is the creation of the Beloved Community."

Clearly, the hundreds of Unitarian Universalist civil rights campaigners who journeyed to Selma, Alabama, felt charged by their local churches to engage in this holy work. These stewards of justice knew that the Beloved Community is rarely embodied in any one place, time, or group, but ever stretches its embrace to include outsiders, strangers, the humiliated, and the marginalized.

The origin of the Beloved Community concept is relatively recent. American philosopher Josiah Royce (1855–1916) coined the phrase in *The Problem of Christianity*,

> Since the office of religion is to aim towards the creation on earth of the Beloved Community, the future task of religion is the task of inventing and applying arts which shall win all over to unity, and which shall overcome their original hatefulness by the gracious love, not of mere individuality but of communities.

In the twentieth century, both Unitarian John Haynes Holmes (1879–1964) and Universalist Clarence Skinner (1881–1949) featured the Beloved Community in their sterling ministries. In fact, Holmes, social activist and minister of Community Church of New York, renamed his parish to exemplify "the practical acknowledgment of religion as the Spirit of Love incarnate in human fellowship." He writes in his autobiography, "the core of its faith, as the purpose of its life, is 'the Beloved Community.'"

Holmes described a vision that spiritual pilgrims have designated variously as the New Jerusalem, the Church Universal, the Glorious Golden City, the Realm of God, or the Peaceable Kingdom. In every case, the Beloved Community extends beyond any particular parish, society, or nation to the very edges of the cosmos, welcoming all of God's creatures into its compassionate embrace.

Skinner, dean of Tufts School of Religion, left several unpublished manuscripts at the time of his death, three of which were gathered into the volume *Worship and a Well-Ordered Life* (1955).

In his chapter "The Church of the Beloved Community," Skinner wrote,

> The Beloved Community is not an organization of individuals seeking private and selfish security for their souls. It is a new adventure, a spontaneous fellowship of consecrated men seeking a new world.

While the worldviews of Holmes and Skinner reflect the post-World War I era in which they ministered, they remain stunningly relevant for any twenty-first–century ecclesiology. Today's Unitarian Universalists might quarrel with their non-associational bent or lack of environmental consciousness, but these two prophetic institutionalists strike a contemporary chord in their insistence that liberal churches operate as democracies, integrating spiritual expression with social witness.

Is there a wider, more inclusive phrase than "Beloved Community" to embrace the global, ecological, congregational, and interpersonal challenges of existence? Can you imagine a more compelling imperative for liberal religion in today's troubled world? King, Holmes, and Skinner all recognized that the Beloved Community was an ideal that could only be approximated during their lifetimes. Accordingly, King used the Beloved Community as a metaphor for a transcendent social order. It represented an unrealized potential here on Earth as well as Heaven itself.

We can grasp the Beloved Community in part but not in full. Although the quest for it transcends generations and history, it also transforms us in the here and now. In our respective corners of the earth, Unitarian Universalists valiantly labor to cultivate enduring sites of belovedness—constantly in need of pruning, ever unfinished. But we know this much to be true: Wherever healthy, vital churches thrive, our chosen religion is contributing its fair share toward the Beloved Community.

Tom Owen-Towle
Spring 2004

Occupy Holy Ground

1

The place where we meet to seek the highest is holy ground.
—Felix Adler

A CHURCH IS NOT A SOCIAL CLUB, a hospital wing, a political action center, or even a spiritual refuge, although all these disparate components are part of what a church is. Rather, healthy congregations are primarily sites for seeking and spreading the holy, however variously referenced by Unitarian Universalist guides: "the deep way" by Unitarian religious educator Sophia Fahs; "the conditions for human transformation" by the Reverend Edward Frost; "centers of redemption" by the Reverend Ralph Stutzman; and "dealing with ultimate things" by the Reverend Barbara Pescan. *Ecclesia* is the Greek word for a regularly convoked assembly. It refers to folks being "called out" of their daily routines for a sacred purpose. *Ecclesia* is not an ethereal entity but a structured, grounded reality. Through church life we embody our holy quest. *Ecclesia* is a chosen kinship circle within which our convictions are refined and our commitments enfleshed. *Ecclesia* is holy ground.

Much of the secular world, other religious denominations, and we Unitarian Universalists ourselves have characterized, if not caricatured, our free faith as every kind of psycho-social-political venture except a religious one. On the contrary, a healthy congregation broaches "serious things in a serious place," in the words of Phillip Larkin, an English agnostic who thought the Anglican faith essentially irrelevant yet knew that churches should engage ultimate concerns—that they should be religious.

This doesn't mean that churches don't interact regularly with the wider society. And we do in fact harbor individuals who promote offbeat philosophical notions and exhibit unconventional behavior. But we are and always have been unapologetically religious. It would appall our Unitarian and Universalist forebears to be perceived, either outside or within our walls, as a nonreligious enterprise. From this day forward, we must begin to view ourselves as a community that, while maverick, unusual, and occasionally revolutionary, is still unashamedly "religious."

And what does it mean to assert that healthy congregations are "holy"? It means we create an environment where minds are stimulated, hearts fortified, souls plumbed, consciences goaded, bodies embraced, and spirits restored. It means that we seek to serve whole human beings, acknowledging that the hallowed is present amid the ordinary and the commonplace.

Holiness doesn't imply that we major in piety or esoteric ritual. And if any Unitarian Universalist traveler should be caught acting "holier than thou," for goodness sake, call her back into line. We have no right to be arrogant or smug about anything, especially in matters religious.

Rather, being holy invites us

- to be still and know that our lives have come into being through and are sustained by a loving Spirit beyond our control, beyond even our comprehension.

- to gather in song and enjoy music as a spiritual expression rather than solely as performance.

- to reach out and physically touch another person, acknowledging that we are accompanied by others on our odyssey.

- to be comforted when our hearts are heavy-laden and awakened when our spirits slumber in indifference.

- to participate in a community of memory and hope where the weightier matters of life are tackled.

Microsoft chairman Bill Gates brags that "he doesn't go to church because it isn't an efficient use of time." Gates is right, if efficiency means simply making money, cranking out a product, or grabbing quick pleasure. But there are many in modern society who hunger for renewal beyond efficiency and for meaning beyond machines—who desperately want to be human beings, not merely human doings. And that process requires religion. The holy is seldom efficient, but it is oh so sustaining.

The Jews who created the Sabbath consciously set time aside to remember that technology and material goods are made for humanity, not we for them. The Sabbath is a time out of time, an opportunity to free ourselves from stress and productivity, to liberate ourselves from our drive and our greed. In Jewish tradition, even the ox is released from toil on the Sabbath. Every creature, human or animal, is respected for its individual essence and given a day of peace. The Sabbath furnishes the pause between the notes in a fine piece of music; without pauses, music isn't all it's meant to be. Without pauses, neither are our lives.

Healthy congregations are also holy in the sense that they are filled with believing folks, parishioners seeking to clarify and deepen their religious convictions. The truth is that Unitarian Universalists believe as heartily and profoundly as members of any other religious fold, but our ways of believing don't scrunch neatly into classic dogmas. We must scuttle, once and for all, the pernicious notion that Unitarian Universalists are people who will either believe anything or believe nothing. Our Unitarian Universalist tradition is rich with sacred affirmations that uphold us: the essential goodness of humankind; the notion that we are held in the grasp of universal, divine, albeit unfathomable, love; the spiritual necessity of living the democratic process; our right to search freely and responsibly for deeper truth and meaning in our lives; our obligation to extend justice and mercy to all living beings; the hope that we can create a peaceful and united world; the authority of conscience, nurtured by reason, intuition, and personal experience; and, many more positive principles that inform and inspire our daily lives. To be sure, the theological differences among us boggle the mind. We range from mystics to humanists to pagans, and wild combinations thereof. We respond differently to various symbols and modes of spiritual practice. We sing differently, reason differently, feel things differently, vote differently. Unitarian philosopher Ralph Waldo Emerson put our condition aptly: "If two people think exactly alike, one of them isn't thinking!"

A healthy congregation works diligently to keep its members believing in wise and compassionate ways. It does so by challenging its stakeholders to address such critical questions as how, when, where, and in whom we believe.

How might we believe? A mature church summons us to freely examine and evaluate every notion that comes our way, keeping as tenets of faith only that wisdom that proves truthful to ourselves, caring toward others, and respectful of the planet. We cannot violate the findings of our conscience and long remain Unitarian Universalists.

When and where do we believe? All the time and everywhere. Our believing is shallow, even phony, if it's reserved only for special occasions and places. Mature Unitarian Universalist congregations charge their members to integrate beliefs and behaviors. They remind parishioners that the religious drive cuts across all phases of human life. It's not a slice of existence, like a section of *Time* magazine. Our religious orientation should be evident in our workplace, in our relationships, and in the performance of our civic duties, as well as during all our church encounters. In church meetings, for example, healthy congregations find that business is conducted more compassionately, even swiftly, when meetings are opened with moments of meditation, a centering thought, and brief but soulful check-ins around the circle.

Finally, in whom do we believe? Significant others, external powers, traditions, ourselves, holy spirits of assorted natures? All of these and more! Unitarian Universalists draw on the wisdom and support of resources outside ourselves—human teachings as well as divine companions—but ultimate responsibility for the moral tenor and spiritual depth of our lives rests with us, as we are companioned, critiqued, and cared for by our chosen Beloved Community.

A healthy church is grounded. The question asked of Adam by God was one of religious geography, after he had sinned and was wandering the Garden: "Where art thou?" This timeless query must be thoughtfully answered by every wayfarer, since locating where we are and asking where we need to be enables us to describe who we are. Geography defines our spirituality. It grounds us. As religious beings, we have no choice but to concern ourselves not only with questions of who I am, with whom I shall travel, and what my duty and joy are while on earth but also with questions of location. Where am I? Where am I in relation to the soil, the sky, the animals and plants, the deities and society? Certainly, we're both wanderers and dwellers, a people of the way and a people with an address. Both sides of the paradox possess wisdom; however, the emphasis on "staying put" isn't as adventurous or romantic-sounding as "taking to the road" and demands stronger advocacy in current society. An accurate translation of the first beatitude in the Christian scriptures reads, "Blessed are they who are at home in the spirit!" Our human goal is to be at home in this singular universe, both physically and spiritually—to know where we truly are and where we're headed. And the most fulfilling place to learn that is in the bosom of our local tribe of free faith.

Our chosen church is our principal tilling ground, sacred ground, battleground, common ground, and growing ground. Yet, in our own congregations, we continue to hear members applaud personal spirituality while denigrating organized religion. They point to the obvious excesses and abuses of institu-

tions. Unitarian Universalist minister Gary James offers a convincing rejoinder in his article "Why 'Organized' Religion":

> These same people would not say, 'I believe in medicine but
> I do not believe in medical schools, hospitals, and clinics.'
> Nor would they say, 'I believe in law and justice but I do not
> believe in law schools, courts and police.' Nor, 'I love art and
> beauty, but I do not believe in art schools and museums.'
> If medicine, justice and art are worth fostering, there must
> be institutions devoted to those purposes. And so it is with
> religion.

Put baldly: Unitarian Universalism is a religion, and religion
is not personal but institutional spirituality. Of course, institutions are—and always will be—complicated, messy, and in need
of constant mending. But that's precisely why we need the interweaving participation of pulpit and pew. Entrusted with the
shared ministry of Unitarian Universalism, we're not permitted to
be freelance philosophers or roving prophets. Ecclesiology
requires that we be active web-builders and web-tenders.

A cosmic "declaration of interdependence" has little relevance
unless religious professionals and laity incarnate what Channing
called "the sense of vast connections" in our daily duties and
tribes. We are charged to serve values beyond our own "compulsive little egos," to use William James' biting expression. If God is
"ultimate concern" or "the ground of being," as theologian Paul
Tillich suggested, then a healthy local church furnishes a site
where human beings can cultivate a relationship with such ulti-
macy and groundedness.

Throughout the sweep of our heritage there has existed a
creative tension between autonomy and community. Yet in a sermon to divinity school alumni, the nineteenth-century Unitarian
minister and organizational genius Henry Whitney Bellows con-
tended that we "have a great deal more obligation to the visible
than to the invisible church. The invisible church takes due care of
itself and of us; the visible church is committed to our hands . . .

the visible church is our charge, because of the two, it alone is within our voluntary reach." Bellows held "that every radically important relationship of humanity is, and must be embodied, in an external institution." And, for him, the primary institutions were family, society, state, and church.

Although the vision and practice of early and medieval Christians were far more exclusionary and intolerant of differing religious views than we are, their ground-floor Latin dictum— *Extra ecclesiam nulla salus*—("outside the church there is no salvation")—points to a profound truth: Holiness is most nearly approximated through experiencing the fullness of the Beloved Community in all its multifarious forms—from local parish to the global whole.

Welcome 2 All Souls

We affirm that every one of us is held in Creation's hand—
a part of the interdependent cosmic web—and hence
strangers need not be enemies; that no one is saved until we
All are saved where All means the whole of Creation.

—William Schulz

THE MISSION OF EVERY Unitarian Universalist community is to
offer an open door to all souls, then to lovingly attend to those
who choose to join our household. Outsiders are kindly welcomed and sensitively treated once inside.

Consequently, extending the hand of fellowship, combined
with steadfast caregiving, comprises the hospitable rhythm of a
vital community of faith. Growth happens, both statistically and
spiritually, when we dare to be what Theodore Parker called a wide
place as well as a warm one. Our congregations would do well to
simply stand for broad acceptance, full inclusion, and communal
salvation, as our Unitarian and Universalist forebears did.

Mature church life begins with hospitality, the most ancient
religious rite, hallowed in every tradition—at least in writ, if less
successfully in practice. Muslim theology holds that on the
proverbial Day of Judgment, humans must give an accounting of
all expenditures except those related to hospitality, which God
would be ashamed to demand.

Regrettably, the art of hospitality in modern culture has been rendered quaint and ineffectual. But in its truest form it is more far-reaching than general civility and table manners. Did you hear about the bishop who kept his files marked "Sacred" and "Top Sacred"? Practicing hospitality is a top sacred venture.

Religious liberals contend that all of us, in one way or another, at one time or another, are the caves in which others find shelter and kinship and they in us, through the ritual bond of hospitality. Friends and strangers, hosts and guests—we are one humanity groping toward the Beloved Community, where we will hear everyone's voice and see everyone's face.

It's tempting, in the name of religious community, to cast people as saints or sinners. But an open-hearted faith like ours complicates matters. Unitarian Universalism insists there's health in the most troublesome parishioners and demonic potential in the most prized among us.

During intergenerational camps at de Benneville Pines Retreat Center in the Southern California mountains, our church often plays a game that underscores our faith commitment to universal respect: reverencing everyone without idolizing anyone. Each person has the name of some well-known Unitarian Universalist pinned on his or her back by the game leaders. We then stroll around the lodge, asking questions about the people whose names we can't see on our own backs—simple yes-no queries such as the gender and era of the person. Most of these names are of the famous Unitarian Universalist variety, but we also mix in names of camp attendees, young and old alike. It always brings a shock of delight and pride when someone learns they're wearing their own name or that of another church camper. The point of the game is crystal clear even to the youngest in our camp: despite our imperfections, we are all beautiful and capable individuals. We belong to a Beloved Community that believes unreservedly in every one of us and affirms that we can be and do marvelous things during our sojourn on earth.

Some wag quipped that some faiths focus on all saints and others on all souls, but Unitarian Universalism is a faith of all sorts. It's a line that draws an understandable chuckle, for we are a fairly unorthodox crew in terms of our philosophies and lifestyles. The bottom line is that we are an intentionally diverse community, encompassing all sorts of souls. Consequently, it should come as little surprise that more of our Unitarian Universalist churches bear the name "all souls" than any other moniker. For we are interested in saluting not only the greats of our own heritage but also the last, the lost, and the least of all humanity. We believe that salvation is for everyone or no one. The Universalist side of our tradition posits an Infinite Spirit that holds every creature in loving embrace. Universalism excludes no one. Our Unitarian side has a compatible emphasis, affirming the inherent worth and supreme dignity of every person, contending that even the shaggiest and shadiest among us are redeemable. Our stubborn belief in the bedrock preciousness of individuals ought never be taken for granted: it is not shared in large portions of the world, and it is frequently threatened by bigotry and intolerance here in America. It remains a distinctive, critical hallmark of our way of doing church.

Church hospitality relates to larger questions of salvation as well. If someone approaches a Unitarian Universalist and pointedly inquires, "Are you saved?" we're likely to respond in one of several ways: "I don't know; it's not my call to make. A greater power than I will need to render that judgment!" Or: "You shouldn't take my word for it. I could tell you anything, so here are some references to check out. These folks will give you a more rounded assessment of the kind of person they sense me to be." Or, "Our faith claims that 'am *I* saved?' isn't the right question to ask or answer. A more relevant one is: 'Are *we* saved?' We affirm that human regard should embrace a larger reality than our own hides. In short, liberal religion focuses upon universal rather than individual salvation."

As practicing Unitarian Universalists, how are members of your congregation prepared to answer that question? Do your church's literature and programs help members to address concerns of hospitality and salvation?

Three main psycho-social dynamics are in play when newcomers enter our church gates. Healthy parishes attend to all three. Whether expressed out loud or not, people are concerned about matters of inclusion, control, and affection. Issues of *inclusion* ask, Will I be welcome? What will be required of me if I join this tribe? Who is missing in this sanctuary? Why? Issues of *control* lift up equally germane queries: How does this community really run? How is power wielded and distributed? Who has influence? And who is helpless? Issues of *affection* ask, Is this church basically a warm or cold place? Is there an inner circle or an interweaving spiral of leaders? Would this congregation miss me if I didn't show up three weeks in a row? And if they did miss me, what would they do about it?

Every healthy church constantly wrestles with these matters. The resolutions won't always prove agreeable or come easily, but co-partners in mature churches tend to stick around rather than drop out. They face off, fight fairly, but seldom flee. Staunch members are ready and willing to help mold and be molded by the curious tribe with which they've cast their lot, for better or for worse.

In the First UU Church of San Diego, we regularly said (or had printed) the following affirmation at the beginning of our worship service:

> Welcome, one and all, to our Unitarian Universalist religious community. We welcome you, whoever you are, whatever tradition, gender, race, sexual orientation, or age you represent. In our presence may you walk the ways of truthfulness, service, and holiness. And through all your days and nights in our presence may you experience love.

On paper, this is a pretty solid statement, but in reviewing it recently, I noted two oversights. First, we left out class, an often ignored category, particularly given the homogenous economic status of most Unitarian Universalists. And "may you walk" assumes that everyone is able-bodied. There are persons in every congregation who aren't. *Move* would have been a better word than *walk*. At a peace rally in town, I remember singing the verse of Pat Humphrey's protest song "We've got to keep on walking forward . . ." and the person next to me was in a wheelchair. Immediately following the song, she boldly shouted, "Not me, not me—I'm movin', but I won't be walkin'!"

Clearly, one could ferret out some flaw in the well-intentioned welcoming words or mission statements found in any of our liberal churches. We repeatedly fall short of our noblest ideals. Our goal remains to become, without growing obsessive, gradually more inclusive—paying sincere attention to who might be left out in our hymn or reading selections, board circles, social action efforts—in all of the sundry rituals of congregational life. Healthy congregations discover new ways to be genuinely expansive, realizing that people are fallible and our churches will keep missing the mark.

Newcomers to our Unitarian Universalist fold need to be informed early on that although they will feel affirmed in some of their convictions, many of their entrenched prejudices will be confronted. This is the maddening but necessary paradox we religious liberals must ride: We're accepted as we are even as we're challenged to grow toward whom we might become.

It's crucial to remember that our liberal religion has expanded in recent years to include the souls of animals as well. Tolstoy says the first step on the road to any informed, universal sense of justice is to stop eating animals. It is not necessary for all Unitarian Universalists to become vegetarians. Nonetheless, we can still welcome animals aboard the ark, ask their forgiveness, and enjoy their company. Some of the hardiest churches in our movement are those where animal celebrations and blessings are regularly held and where people who count animals as family are warmly supported.

The sad truth is that, at different times in human history, various classes of beings—be they women, homosexuals, poor folks, persons of color, or some other designated group—have been regarded as creatures without souls in order to justify cruelty. We perpetuate that degrading practice whenever we treat the beasts of the field, the birds of the sky, and the fish of the sea as resources only, without intrinsic value. In the long sweep of moral and spiritual evolution, said fellow Unitarian Charles Darwin, human beings have gradually learned to widen the circle of our compassion for and kinship with other living entities. It's never too late to welcome fellow animals into our sacred communion. "Speciesism" has been learned by us; it can be unlearned.

The Beloved Community, in its fullness, welcomes the whole of Creation. All sorts of souls.

Care for Your Own 3

We must all lean upon others. Let's see that we lean grace-
fully and freely and acknowledge their support.
                                        —Margaret Collier Graham

HOSPITALITY IS STRENUOUS WORK. Some of our congregations
are better than others at welcoming the stranger, but they fail to
meet the needs of existing members, or vice versa. The objective
of a healthy church is to provide a continuum of care from
entrance to exit.

The Rissho Kosei-kai, a liberal Japanese Buddhist movement,
furnishes a useful model. Every member is an active participant in
a small kinship group of challenge and comfort, called a *hoza*.
Hozas exist solely to strengthen the overall "interdependent web"
of a local tribe—soothing members when they're down and prod-
ding them when they're slothful. In Unitarian Universalist parishes, similar groups are variously called *affinity circles, covenant
crews*, and *small group ministries*.

Both outreach and inreach are obligatory for the full-fledged
religious community: Service to the larger world and care of our
own membership. Lest our religion grow lopsided, balanced
Unitarian Universalist parishes sustain an internal caregiving network as varied and vital as their external social action program.
"Love thy neighbor as thyself" means "as much as," not "more or

less than." There's an implied equal sign in that phrase. We can't fully love our neighbor unless we feel at peace with ourselves. Similarly, authentic self-caring impels us to nourish earth and neighbor with overflowing mercy. Love, the genuine article, is utterly indivisible.

Who is my neighbor? In recent times we've fortunately evolved a global consciousness that expands the concept of neighbor to include not only friends and acquaintances but also strangers and foreigners, even non-human beings. At the moment however, we'll concentrate upon those brothers and sisters dwelling in our home congregation. That's a hefty homework assignment in its own right. The sad reality is that Unitarian Universalists, blessed with an aching, ardent prophetic conscience, are often stronger in our social outreach to outcasts in need than in personal inreach to the hurting in our own homes and churches. It's trickier to care up close than from afar. Church family members invariably stick around; society's downtrodden eventually recede from direct view. Plus it's usually more dramatic and satisfying to the ego to march for civil liberties or sign an initiative for reproductive rights than it is to drive a fellow parishioner to worship or take them a hot meal.

Nonetheless, we must never forget that our own fellow churchgoers suffer, regularly and greatly. We tend to think that Unitarian Universalists are fairly comfortable, sane, and self-reliant. Sometimes yes, sometimes no. Any sampling of the humanity inhabiting our liberal religious homes reveals disruption, disease, and death. There isn't a member of any congregation who doesn't also hold membership in the largest fellowship in the world—the communion of those who bear the mark of suffering and pain.

Certainly, studies have shown that people are less likely to commit suicide, be depressed, abuse drugs, or stay sick if they are involved in meaningful community. Just attending church proves statistically healthy for the soul. But parishioners still suffer. In every Unitarian Universalist community there are financial woes, terminal illnesses, runaway youth, victims or perpetrators of sexual violence, and terrible loneliness. There are individuals burdened by chronic mental illness; there are partners separating monthly. Members and friends of our churches are hospitalized, grieving, disabled, facing overwhelming job pressures or loss of employment, home-bound or institutionalized, in the grip of a spiritual crisis or chemically dependent.

In every liberal outpost, adherents are facing an unplanned pregnancy or desperately seeking to get pregnant. Others are experiencing the birth or adoption of a child. Still others feel embattled as single parents. There are members of our flocks who are painfully working through issues of sexual orientation. There are friends to your very right and left in Sunday worship who've been affected by accidental or natural disasters, who've been injured or imprisoned. And many are undergoing the substantial stress of moving to or away from our local church.

A Unitarian Universalist colleague tells the poignant story of her daughter, who tried to commit suicide and was sheltered for a while in a mental health institution. A church friend of the family learned of her plight and went to visit. As she reached down to hug her friend's daughter, the young woman reached upward, stared at the caring face, and seeing the chalice worn around her visitor's neck, firmly clutched it as if she were grasping a life-saving relic. We sometimes overlook the fact that Unitarian Universalism carries healing power both in its artifacts and through our physical presence. In a creedal faith, people are united by common beliefs; in a covenantal faith we are united by mutual caring. We are summoned, in fair or foul weather, to love alike even when we do not believe alike, as Francis David, the founder of Transylvanian Unitarianism, expressed it in the sixteenth century.

Our liberal religious covenant is to trust one another enough to seek help when we're down and to offer assistance when we're able. One of our former members confided, "First Church is one place where, when members ask 'How are you?' they really want to hear the unvarnished truth. It's a real question with caring intent. My church has redeemed my life!" Another member once said, "Whereas I recognize myself to be the primary authority for my life, I need my faith community to chasten, challenge, and comfort me— in short, to *chalice* me!" Every one of our congregations could recount stories in which members, young and old alike, have been on the giving or receiving end of immeasurable healing and hope.

To phrase it biblically, we are members, one with another, of the same body. We are as limbs, and when there is an ache or loss, torment or separation in one of the limbs, our whole body shudders and rallies to restore equilibrium. We can't save one another from anguish, but we can serve one another in the throes of it.

Healthy congregations recognize the purpose and power of a caregiving network, and each will sculpt its own form, structure, and way of caregiving. It might be launched with a sermon, followed by a survey, personal interviews, and perhaps a town meeting. Usually there's a committee, a team, even a staff person who coordinates a clearinghouse for the visits, phone calls, transportation, and support needs of the overall congregation. In every congregation there are both caregivers and those who need care. Members are urged to be both strong enough to give and vulnerable enough to accept help. Most importantly, the caregivers in the network are neither outsider counselors nor paid consultants but congregational peers. So no one can say, "I'll let the caregiving crew do the compassionate inreach in my church," any more than pledge drive canvassers give all the money themselves. We are a religious cooperative and need the hearts and hands of everyone in our family ready to care as appropriate. Every Sunday, the network staffs the patio, the vestibule, the coffee hour—ever on the alert for expressed or unexpressed cries circulating in the congregation. Caregivers can't afford just to hug their buddies after service; they are beckoned to extend a hand to the stranger whose face reveals despondency or whose walk betrays a hurt. A church's caregiving team is particularly responsive, following the service, to those individuals who may have voiced specific joys or concerns during the worship hour.

Furthermore, although it's easy to do, we dare not forget those members who are housebound, who will rarely, if ever, darken the door of their Beloved Community again, yet who still fervently crave communion. As one pivotal leader in the ranks of her home church told me recently, more with puzzlement than bitterness, "Now that I'm aging and finally need some caregiving myself, where is it?"

Additionally, there are moments in the yearly liturgical life when caregivers are both charged and thanked, and those who need care are emboldened to seek assistance from their spiritual kin. In truth, natural caregiving should take place every time we meet to transact business, hold classes, do social outreach, or share worship. For, at the end of our earthly existence, we will not be asked, "How much do you know?" or "How magnificent is your steeple?" but simply "How deeply did you care about the sisters and brothers whom you were blessed to meet both within and without the walls of your church?"

A caregiving program is not a passing fancy but an ongoing commitment in the life of the shared ministry of a Unitarian Universalist society. The network will periodically break down and need to be patched, sometimes rebuilt. Large, small and medium-sized congregations need some kind of Caregiving Network—a structured, reliable, enduring program to serve the manifold needs for care, nurturing, and healing of its members. The church staff and religious professionals require it too. Expecting the minister, for example, to be solely responsible for the well-being of a congregation is a burden that both drains clergy and underutilizes laity.

Ministers are trained as professional caregivers and definitely should carry their share of the load. Indeed, perhaps professional ministry was invented to serve as a reminder that such work ought to be done and that up-close caregiving work is never finished. But mature religious professionals eagerly augment the shared ministry with lay pastoral associates in every area of church life, whether it be community action, liturgical leadership, organizational development, or caregiving. Competent clergy refuse to hoard any segment of ministry; they spread it around, multiplying the gifts.

Finally, a resourceful, year-round caregiving network enhances the well-being and growth of the caregivers. Giving care to others in our religious community renews our own souls. The very word *care* has its roots in the old Gothic term *kara*, which means to lament. The real meaning of care, therefore, has to do with grieving, experiencing sorrow, feeling the pain of another, and being present for another. Being a caregiver is both a great privilege and a gift. One word of warning. Healthy churches work diligently to counter *helpaholism*. In short, care*givers* in a church setting must avoid becoming care*takers*. The latter presumes resolving another person's concern. We simply can't do that. Our mission as caregivers is to give steady and appropriate care in the face of stress and loss. I like the way Oliver Wendell Holmes put it: "The physician's task is to cure rarely, relieve often, and comfort always." That's our ecclesiastical mission too. In actuality, a caregiving team isn't going to cure many ills, social or personal. So curing isn't our central aim; caring is.

A mature congregation, while caring, is neither a hospital ward nor a counseling center. It refuses to allow "illness" or "neediness" to define the culture of the parish. Health practitioner Rachel Naomi Remen makes useful distinctions between helping, fixing, and serving. The helping and fixing modes begin from a premise that someone is weak and/or broken, whereas service rests on the premise that we're all connected. Fixing and helping foster distance between people; serving is an intimate matter. You cannot serve remotely. Caregiving is service; caretaking focuses on fixing and helping the wounded.

As caregivers we're willing to show up and offer our support—despite our acknowledged defects—for all of us are wounded healers. Our task is to place our strength next to the weakness of another—on the phone, through a note, or in person. We cannot perform soul transplants, but we can be faithful companions.

Congregations face another caregiving dilemma. Our contemporary society is saturated with recovery movements, many of which have been successful in encouraging people not to try to navigate life as self-reliant troopers, especially when troubled or trapped by a problem tougher than our own wills. Indeed the real estate of Unitarian Universalist congregations across the land houses innumerable such support groups, particularly those who can't find a safe haven elsewhere in town.

However, while persons may understandably prefer to remain in a state of perpetual recovery, it seems appropriate that a religious professional periodically nudge her fellow parishioners to graduate at some point and return to the claims of the larger world. That's where our liberal, liberating religion comes into play. It never permits us to stay stuck in self-recovery. While comforting us, healthy churches don't let us take up permanent residence in a state of comfort. A full-service religious community reminds us that while we are reclaiming our own sanity and inner peace from private demons and pernicious addictions, we're also summoned, as we are able, to do our part in reclaiming society from its equally stubborn injustices and the earth from the clutches of human greed. Aspirants in the Beloved Community must remain vigilant and active on all fronts—personal, relational, global, and spiritual—knowing well that any self-transformation worth pursuing is inextricably interwoven with the restoration of the whole of Creation.

In summary, a church exists to care. When the great philosopher and mystic Baron Von Hugel was dying, his niece bent over because she could see his lips moving but couldn't catch what he said. She put her ear against his mouth and heard the last words Von Hugel ever uttered: "Caring is everything, nothing matters but caring."

Yes, caring is everything. It's our mission as a religious people. Yet sincerely caring for those in our own religious community while allowing them to care for us often proves the slipperiest challenge of all.

Give Everyone a Voice

It's not the symphony of voices in sweet concert I enjoy, but the cacophony of democracy, the brouhahas and the donnybrooks, the full-throated roar of a free people busy using their right to freedom of speech. Democracy requires rather a large tolerance for confusion and a secret relish for dissent. This is not a good country for those who are fond of unanimity and uniformity.

—Molly Ivins

To MOLLY IVINS' COMMENT, I would add: Neither is mature congregational life for those fond of perpetual harmony and sameness. Our tenacious Unitarian Universalist commitment to the way of democracy begins and ends in faithfulness to the undiminished equality of human beings before the Infinite Spirit.

Democracy stands in deep alignment with our heritage and principles. Unitarian Universalist minister Alice Blair Wesley writes, "Show me the patterns of your church organization, and I'll show you what the people of the church find worthiest of their loyalty. Organization and theology are not two different things. Our organization is a function of our actual theology."

The word *democracy* comes from *demos* (people) and *cracy* (rule) in our congregational life. Too few people ruling is one dilemma; everybody in charge is another. For democracy to flourish, we need the delicate synthesis of sufficient numbers of people actively and constructively wielding power. Such is the quest of the Beloved Community.

We belong to the tradition of nonconformists who rebuffed the established church in England, asserting that God was unimpressed by either academic degrees or ecclesiastical appointments, let alone measures such as material wealth or state power. As our Unitarian ancestor Theodore Parker—later quoted by Abraham Lincoln—said, ours is a faith "of the people, by the people and for the people."

Accordingly, each of our freethinking congregations is governed not by the whim of charismatic clergy or a distant diocese or even a heavenly mandate. We are run by our membership: the people. Some wit noted, "The liberal church is too important to be left in the hands of the laity." Another countered with, "The church is too important to be left in the hands of the clergy." There exists a necessary, third option: "Our progressive faith is simply too important to be left behind, and will always require the collaborative gifts of both pulpit and pew." As a result, Unitarian Universalism heeds the imperative to embody a shared ministry at every level of church existence.

The great nineteenth-century Danish theologian Sören Kierkegaard remarked that most parishioners think that God is the director of this play called "life," that the minister is a lead actor, and that the congregation is the audience. But Kierkegaard countered this perception with his own analysis: The congregants are the actors, God is the audience, and ministers are the prompters, supplying forgotten lines.

The job of a religious professional, then, is to lift up the duties and destinies—the dramatic lines, if you will—that parishes tend to forget or lose sight of. Ministers are to recall the lines that call us to our highest and holiest selves, filled with enormous promise to make Creation more beautiful and just and loving.

Each of our chosen congregations is a potentially mighty group, full of power and purpose. We are also fragile enterprises, full of lethargy and nastiness. We are both. As Paige Getty, the former intern minister at First Unitarian Universalist Church in San Diego, described it, "Well, it sure appears to me that First Church is a healthily imperfect group!"

Yet through it all—clashes, celebrations, and heartaches—we pledge to remain companions on the spiritual path. Companions are literally "those who [willingly sit down together and talk and] share bread." A robust church is a companionable family of all ages and backgrounds, orientations and classes—seeking truth, seeking to serve, seeking to be carriers of holiness. Democracy in its religious form is a shared ministry.

As it was phrased in our weekly order of service,

> We envision members and friends of First Church as pilgrims traveling on life's journey together—creating shared ministry through which we can grow our souls in ways truthful to ourselves, caring of others, and sustaining of the planet.

Therefore, whether in governance, liturgy (literally, "the work of the people"), or in religious growth and learning, Unitarian Universalist ecclesiology testifies that each person's ideas and gifts are valued. As Unitarian forebear Theodore Parker phrased it, "Democracy means not I am as good as you are, but you are as good as I am." Note the emphasis on equality rather than ego, on our neighbor before ourselves.

One of our subtler Unitarian Universalist Principles, often underplayed in congregational deliberations, is our staunch commitment to "the rights of conscience." In democratic parish life, this means that while each of us listens to and learns from other church stakeholders, but we hold the final responsibility for how we act, given what we know and who we are. Our liberal faith tradition boldly challenges society to choose democracy in matters religious. It's no modest spiritual achievement to stay a course where power is shared equally and everyone is answerable.

Gertrude Stein once said about Paris, "It's not what Paris gives you; it's what she doesn't take away." We can't give our membership everything. We can't possibly meet everyone's grandest fantasies or desires, nor should we even try. Nonetheless, when the chips are down, Unitarian Universalism can promise members and friends an accepting, open home in which to cultivate our consciences.

Simply put, our individual consciences—informed, compassionate, and always fallible—remain in creative tension with the directives of both our government and our congregation. Therefore, we're charged to cheer nation and/or faith when they seem worthy of praise, to criticize them when they fall short, and to comfort them when they stand in need of consolation. Occasionally, our conscience prompts us to do all three simultaneously.

At this juncture, let's visit an example of democracy at work in local church life, namely, the sticky area of political and patriotic diversity. All Unitarian Universalists are not progressives and radicals, conventional opinion to the contrary; there are plenty of political conservatives and moderates in every one of our congregations. Mature churches do address sociopolitical issues, but never in a partisan fashion. There's no single, right way to be a patriot—that is, a loyal lover of one's country—in our ecclesiastical ranks. Hence, a truly liberal congregation is called to be a house of forthright and diverse opinion, one that welcomes a potpourri of patriots.

One of our San Diego church's proudest moments occurred during the Persian Gulf War in 1991, when we simultaneously provided deployment blues support groups for families of those serving in the Gulf and protest opportunities for those who opposed the war. I had been a founding member of our local Peace Resource Center back in 1975, yet I remained ardently dedicated to patriotic diversity in our congregational ranks. While I was preaching a sermon on the Gulf War, voicing open opposition to our government's military engagement, one of our church members—dressed in full military regalia—stood during the entire worship service, some twenty feet from the pulpit, in full view of the congregation, signaling his commitment to waging a "just war."

Phillip approached me immediately after the service and declared with a tearful embrace, "Our entire church approach, including your sermon today, hasn't driven either me or my family out! As a military man, I can still worship here as a Unitarian Universalist. Hallelujah to our conscious acceptance of deep differences!" We then walked arm-in-arm from the sanctuary to our meeting hall, to share in a congregation-wide airing of divergent patriotic concerns.

Democracy holds sway in our theology, ethics, and lifestyles; it should triumph in our political and patriotic stances as well. That's why the task force at First Church has been called "Peace and Democracy" to remind folks that our faith tradition calls for religious democracy in practice and that every patriotic voice seeking sincere expression will and must be heard if our outpost aspires to resemble "belovedness."

There are rights, rites, responsibilities, and risks associated with becoming a member of the democratic enterprise that is a local Unitarian Universalist outpost. Joining a Unitarian Universalist society gives one the opportunity to vote on ecclesiastical concerns as well as to chair committees and organizations. Members become outright stakeholders.

But the process of becoming a member in too many of our societies lacks the necessary seriousness. Each congregation must contrive its own set of procedures, but suffice it to say that the more intentional and thorough, the better. Possibilities for significant integration might include: membership classes; an hourlong meeting with one or more of the religious professionals, followed by a session with lay leaders where opportunities to pledge and serve are delineated; a membership book signing and/or worship service litany; and a church-wide reception.

Then, to make sure new members don't drop out quickly, it's wise to contact them shortly after they join to make sure they've connected with friendly members and fulfilling tasks. Periodic reunions of discrete membership classes have proven useful too.

Voting is a sacred rite; thus, one of the holy events of a church year is the annual fiscal meeting. Unitarian Universalist congregations aren't run by the Association leadership in Boston, by a synod, or by the resident clergy. We're governed strictly by our own membership, in a polity that comes about as close as one can get to a religious version of participatory democracy. It was seen as heresy when our Unitarian and Universalist forebears permitted—even required—every congregation to transact its own spiritual and financial business.

I remember when our young son Russ asked, "Who owns the church?" I think he sort of hoped that his parents—both ministers —did, so that, by virtue of his blood lines, he might too some day. Russ was crestfallen when we announced that it belonged to some several hundred people, and smartly retorted, "Well, it sure doesn't seem like it!"

We Unitarian Universalists aren't the masters of our fate in some absolute way, but neither are we powerless victims. We're free to responsibly render good enough decisions that will make our personal and congregational lives more worthwhile. So when our faith tradition says it believes in us, it earnestly does. Our religious vocation, then, is to seize the God-given capacity to be a choice-maker—to show up, discuss and debate, and vote our conscience on the decisions of our chosen family.

When we join one of our democratic Unitarian Universalist clans, we're also entitled to share in a vast panoply of ceremonies and rites of passage—personal, relational, and communal. There are the standard commemorations of birth, coming-of-age, partnership, and death. Rites that welcome and say farewell to members are routine as well. Choir-tribute Sundays, religious education leadership recognition, and age-appropriate transitional celebrations are common. And there are countless other familiar rites of passage.

But healthy congregations are inventive, spawning fresh rites relevant to their particular context, such as "wholly family" services that lift up and celebrate all configurations of devoted and committed intimates; credos and testimonies; and support rites for relational breakups.

And then there are those ceremonies that uphold the contributions of members to the church community, some of which can appropriately be considered liturgical moments and therefore celebrated during the worship service. Unitarian Universalist of the Year awards for either service to the church or to the larger community come to mind. Unsung Unitarian Universalists can be paid tribute as well, often at a luncheon that follows worship. In San Diego, we also honor one individual a year with the Shameless Agitator Award, given on a designated Social Action Sunday.

One of the trickier, yet duly appropriate, rites occurs whenever we give parishioners a well-deserved sabbatical from church duty, recognizing that they will prove hardier supporters upon their return to service. We say thank you for what they've already done and offer our heartfelt encouragement of their time of rest and renewal, as each honored congregant becomes a recipient for a time, rather than a giver. Healthy churches remember that laity need sabbaticals too. If honestly created and honorably conducted, there can rarely be an overabundance of such sacred passages.

There's the story of the great nineteenth-century liberal minister from Boston, Phillips Brooks, who was about to embark for Europe. A friend jokingly suggested that he might bring a new religion back with him, and cautioned Brooks to be careful if he did, for it might be difficult to get a new religion through the Customs House. "I doubt it," Brooks replied. "In all likelihood, any new religion popular enough to import to this land would have no duties attached to it!"

Well, our Unitarian Universalist religion, at its most authentic, has duties, plenty of them, but they are freely chosen, not externally imposed. I've grown to realize that Unitarian Universalists are the type of folks who wish to be challenged. People increasingly come to our congregations not merely to be fed but to feed others. They're searching for ways to be held accountable—personally, vocationally, and prophetically. They want to learn how to walk the tightrope between giving themselves over to an institution and giving themselves away—the distinction between healthy surrender and crippling subjugation.

Once in the course of a lengthy memorial tribute, a minister paused, bent over the wreaths of flowers, pointed to the draped casket below, and with lowered voice and an exceedingly solemn face intoned, "Ladies and gentlemen, dearly beloved of the Lord," and he thrust his finger downward, and, in Freudian fashion, declared, "This member was a corpse in our church for twenty years!" May that verdict never be rendered concerning our respective church tenures.

Finally, I always like to alert newcomers to the risks involved in becoming a church-subscribing Unitarian Universalist. I warn them that in joining our local congregation, they run the risk of becoming so enthusiastic about the purposes of this faith that an irresistible urge may arise to tell their friends and associates about it. They may even end up passing out pamphlets on street corners. Or at the very least, their daily decisions may be noticeably influenced by their newfound faith.

Mature church leaders realize that religion isn't a bean supper as much as a partisan fray. We must take sides, make discerning choices, join up and join in those institutions we cherish. The American poet Carl Sandberg became a committed member of the Unitarian Church in Asheville, North Carolina. His exhortation from a church newsletter rings true:

> You can't go tramping around from church to church and build anything up. Who would want to go on a picnic all the time and eat out of other people's baskets? You've got to feel the importance of your own individual participation in its life.

Every Wednesday we've had the privilege of taking care of one of our three young grandchildren, Trevor, Corinne, and Owen, who blessedly live nearby in San Diego. Together we've engaged in little rituals that appeal to one or the other of us. One of our normal routines is singing and/or dancing to folk and campfire melodies. A family favorite is the Hokey-Pokey. You know the drill: "You put your right foot in, you put your right foot out, you put your right foot in, and you shake it all about; You do the hokey-pokey and you turn yourself around, that's what it's all about." The kids really hurl their bodies into this routine.

The Hokey-Pokey starts with the right foot, goes through most of our limbs, then ends up with "you put your whole self in, you put your whole self out, you put your whole self in and you shake it all about; You do the hokey-pokey and you turn yourself around. That's what it's all about."

I've come to recognize that the Hokey-Pokey is a fine metaphor for mature congregational commitment. We start by sticking our toes into the stream of Unitarian Universalism. If we can stand the temperature, we venture further in until we end up plunging into the flowing river of this responsibly free religion. Such serious, whole-bodied participation is truly what it's all about—in family, in religion, in life itself.

Who of us really wants to come to the end of our journey and realize that we've been little more than a spectator on the sidelines, a toe-tester, a yes-butter, only partially committed to those communities that are safe and saving for us and all whom we touch? To summarize the overlapping four Rs of rights, rites, responsibilities, and risks, here are excerpts from a Membership Ceremony in San Diego:

> We are happy you are with us. We gladly share with you in everything that strengthens this congregation. And we stand with you against anything that will injure or weaken it.

> We believe that membership in our Beloved Community will enrich and enlarge your life as well as ours. We want your gifts. We offer you ours. Know well that in our membership you are truly accepted to come as you are and to grow who you wish to become.

Naturally, there are additional relevant Rs in the fostering of a mature congregation, such as *repentance, resistance,* and *reconciliation.* Numerous others will undoubtedly come to your mind.

Encourage Unity Amidst Diversity

What is our oneness? We need to celebrate the whole as well
as the parts. How can we become One . . . in commitment to
collaborative, connecting community?

—Diane Olson

OUR AMERICAN MOTTO endures: *e pluribus unum* ("out of many,
one"). Yet religious liberty and diversity are under alarming attack
by uniformity-seeking religious extremists. To them, reaching different conclusions about moral and spiritual matters is unaccept-
able. Pluralism is considered a sin.

There is a precarious balance between the one and the many
in our land, both politically and religiously. To function effective-
ly we need to be one nation, indivisible—united states. We must
share common values and a mutual dedication to our system of
government. But our country should never blur the many cultures, races, religions, and ideologies therein. Our peculiar
strength resides in our tremendous pluralism. E pluribus unum.

The key in healthy churches is the ability to ride as intrepid-
ly as possible this dynamic paradox of unity amidst diversity. No
congregation does this flawlessly. Nonetheless, in a flourishing
Unitarian Universalist parish all living traditions and theologies
are duly honored; and different classes, colors, capacities, and
life choices are welcomed. The goal is to be diverse without

becoming divided, to grow unified without succumbing to uniformity.

To become an ever-maturing congregation, it's prudent to track several areas of commonality. First, a healthy church exhibits a common memory that includes yet transcends its current stakeholders. Present-day Unitarian Universalists exist in relationship to previous heretics and change agents, institutionalists and reformers who are the religious ancestors of us all. A healthy parish is conscious of standing in a stream of Unitarian Universalist exemplars both from near and far and regularly pays homage to their legacies and legends, even naming rooms or endowing programs in their honor.

The opening of the second act of Gilbert and Sullivan's *Pirates of Penzance* shows Major-General Stanley ("the very model of the modern major-general . . .") apologizing to the ancestors buried in the chapel yard of his estate for having besmirched the family honor by lying to the pirates. To escape their clutches, he's told them that, like them, he's an orphan. Another character asks the Major-General why he's apologizing to the tombstones, who aren't his ancestors at all—why, he "only bought the property a year ago" They are in fact his ancestors, Stanley replies, because they came with the property when he bought it.

Universalist and Unitarian pioneers like Hosea Ballou, Judith Murray Sargent, Whitney Young, and Mary Livermore are our spiritual ancestors, along with the our predecessors in our own particular congregations. They came with the property when we bought or inherited it. When we speak or fail to speak the truth in love, these spiritual ancestors stand in the wings, reassuring or chastising us on cue.

First Unitarian Universalist Church of San Diego displays several reminders of its forebears. There is a memorial wall bearing the names of its ancestors on removable tablets, each with full name and birth and death dates, those dignified equalizers. And every Easter morning, the names of those who've died during the preceding year are reverentially acknowledged, along with the births of babies.

There is also a Greeting Garden, an outdoor center for meditation and renewal. It's graced with this inscription from Christopher Wren: "If you would see their monuments, look around you," and goes on to read, "Honoring those who made possible the establishment in 1959 and the expansion in 1987 of this Unitarian Universalist center of spiritual freedom."

Additionally, in Balboa Park, where thousands of people stroll weekly, First Church, along with our denomination's other local outposts, paid for twelve flowering peach trees and three park benches. Each is marked with plaques that read, "Given by the Unitarian Universalist congregations of San Diego in commemoration of 125 years of religious freedom."

These visible markers keep the common memory of Unitarian Universalism alive and well in our particular corner of the land. What concrete reminders enable your specific parish and parishioners to be remembered?

A vital church also forges a common vision, answering the questions of why are we here and what shall we do together. From this vision emerges a concise mission statement, followed by goals, norms, and objectives by which the community covenants to dwell together. The key is for each local congregation to locate, declare, and bring alive our core of common values, recognizing that without a vision the people perish.

A Beloved Community also gathers, over time, common relics such as the flaming chalice to serve as unifying symbols. The chalice (since its adoption in 1941 by the Unitarian Service Committee) symbolizes the blaze of freedom, the light of truth, the fire of action, and the warmth of community. We currently see it around necks and on nightstands, in sanctuaries and in classrooms, cherished by children, youth, and adults alike. Whenever Unitarian Universalists spot the flaming chalice, we know we're at home and we gather on common ground.

Although liturgical forms differ from congregation to congregation, laity and religious professionals collaborate in shaping a common worship. Worship holds the primary place in parish life, because it unites where beliefs naturally divide. Worship occasions a circle of interlocked arms and interpenetrating minds meshing in common aspiration.

At its finest, worship can do for the soul what sleep does for the body: It can strengthen and invigorate our lives. It can inspire— "breathe fresh life"—into our very beings. Genuine worship addresses the primary dimensions of the bounteous religious journey: reaching within through personal enrichment, reaching without through social witness, and reaching beyond through spiritual devotion. On any given Sunday, worshippers may be readier to reach in one direction than in another. Yet sometimes all three movements occur, resulting in a glorious epiphany.

But why have communal worship anyway? Why not just rely upon spontaneous, solitary communion with God or nature? Corporate worship brings us sustenance when we're hurting. And it shakes us up when we're smug. It's tougher to compromise your soul when Unitarian Universalist companions are constantly needling and nurturing you.

No one prays the Lord's Prayer in the first person singular: "Give *me* this day my daily bread. . . ." Rather, it's the petition of a Beloved Community. "Give *us* this day our daily bread." We are dependent for our daily bread upon one another, upon hundreds of strangers whom we'll never meet. I can't grow wheat, I don't package it, or deliver it to myself. There's a greater cycle of which I am but a part. Therefore, I need to give back something in exchange for that. If we let each other down, our humanity withers, our religion fails, the interdependent web frays.

This is as true for spiritual as for physical bread. Many are the times we come to church out of sorts, unexpectant, dull, angry; and then something or someone touches our beings in a precious, lasting way. Grace, inspiration—call it what we will—happens. We arrive out of habit, and our lives are altered because of a blessed encounter with the holy.

Healthy congregations celebrate their diversity in addition to cultivating their unity. A mature, vital congregation is one that pursues depth, or the sense of the holy; growth—both inwardly, of the spirit, and outwardly, through evangelism; warmth, or the art of hospitality; and breadth, or intentional diversity, in all its forms. In a world where people's options for growth are constricting, jobs are shrinking, and perspectives are narrowing, a liberal (large-minded and open-hearted) church becomes a critical site for expanding our horizons. In our households of faith, travelers are given sufficient room to explore their own souls to the fullest.

In orders of service across our Unitarian Universalist land-scape, one will often find the phrase "intentionally diverse com-munity." This refers to our shared aspiration to embrace, not merely to tolerate, a range of theologies, lifestyles, orientations, backgrounds, cultures, races, and more.

The quest for diversity extracts two promises from congregants: that we will practice diversity within our own walls, not merely preach it in the wider world; and that we will stay on the path for-ever. Authentic diversity is not an ad hoc project but our way of being and doing religion. We are flawed yet dogged in our commit-ment to all kinds of diversity. On the subject of racial diversity, Bill Jones, one of our leading theologians, goes right to the heart of the challenge: "The mission of racial justice is nothing less than the co-equality of individuals." The concepts of assimilation and inte-gration inadequate to the task, whether one is speaking of race, class, orientation, or ability. Only co-equality will do, honoring as it does the full worth and value of everyone.

Such is the primary socio-ethical question of our times: Can we be different without growing alienated, diverse without being divisive? Diversity leads to dialogue, division leads to oppression. Open-flowing energy between different parties, people, races, church groups, and nations always builds bridges. But when one of the parties listens only long enough to tell the others what to do, to obtain power or superiority, the result is alienation.

"The problem with white liberalism," writes Episcopal priest Carter Heyward (and this directly applies to our Unitarian Universalist congregations), "is that liberal white men and women do not advocate real or mutual relations, but rather a patronizing sort of relation based on hand-me-down affections. White liberals love black people; white liberal men love black women, as long as we're not threatening to change the name of the power game." But co-equality changes the power game—it redistributes resources and equalizes privilege. It calls us to build social justice rather than build personal empires in our local congregations and larger communities.

The word *diversity* betrays us in our quest for the Beloved Community if it becomes but a euphemism for sameness, conveying the erroneous impression that the experiences of all ethnic and racial groups in the United States are virtually interchangeable. As someone has pointedly remarked: "Hey, remember that the slave plantations were diverse but not just." That's why our Association-wide racial justice program, Journey Toward Wholeness, is an anti-racist, multicultural enterprise. The truth persists that even if we never radically alter the racial demographics represented in our predominantly white Unitarian Universalist congregations, we must still actively combat racism.

Lest we become discouraged, even immobilized, on the journey toward wholeness, there are encouraging reminders to keep us on course. First, Unitarian Universalist justice-builders will never be members of any moral majority, but we do belong to what Martin Luther King Jr. called "dedicated minorities." As such, we refuse to be trivialized as fringe folks by those who wish to maintain an inequitable, oppressive status quo.

Unitarian Universalism is by temperament a conciliatory religion, and it's tempting to try to make people like us when we do justice work. But it seldom works that way. Moving beyond racism toward co-equality and full freedom for all will necessarily cost those of us in places of power ample disruption and discomfort. As justice-building congregations, we're not called to feel or look good but to do good. Alma Crawford, minister of the Church of the Open Door in Chicago, likes to say, "Remember discomfort, like fasting, can be a spiritual discipline. So, practice it!"

Every day we're summoned to perform deeds, however minor, on behalf of those who suffer injustice because of their gender, economic status, differing ability, race, and sexual orientation, acknowledging, as Martin Luther King said, that "we must accept finite disappointment, but we must never lose infinite hope . . . for the moral arc of the universe bends toward justice."

Healthy congregations are also committed to religious literacy and in-depth theological thinking. Literacy requires that members become knowledgeable about religion in general and Unitarian Universalism in particular. It's indefensible to define one's convictions primarily in negative rather than affirmative terms. Such behavior merely exhibits prolonged adolescence and stunts our growth as a movement.

Religious adulthood arrives only when we become conversant with and expressive of the bedrock affirmations of both our Unitarian and Universalist heritages. Grounded sufficiently in our traditions, we can then proceed to think theologically about all areas of church life. This theological maturity comes not merely from taking assorted adult religious education courses but from a dedication to making congregational decisions informed by our Principles and Purposes. Religious literacy and theological thinking require sustained energy and alertness all the days of our sojourn in a Unitarian Universalist tribe.

In a similar vein, all our commitments to interfaith cooperation in the larger world (especially in the polarized post-September 11 context) are valuable, but counterfeit, unless we're practicing theological pluralism in our home congregations. Too frequently we experience humanists and theists, for example, chewing one another into bits in our parishes. The lesson is that we need to practice healthier interfaith dialogue in our own households. Then our witness to the larger religious world will be more authentic and credible.

Bedrock acceptance starts by saluting our unity—we are first and foremost *Unitarian Universalists*, a name that denotes the institutional, historical, and religious identity that we hold in common. *Unitarian Universalism* is the noun of our faith; our differing theological persuasions are the adjectival modifiers.

Our congregations need to celebrate the fact that Unitarian Universalism pulls not from one or two religious traditions but from a boundless reservoir of sources. We derive from the mystical and rational traditions, from historical and nature-based religions, indeed from a treasure trove of spiritual insights handed on to us from every corner and era of the world.

Unitarian Universalism boldly declares that diversity is the reality of our contemporary world and that attempting to establish a monolithic culture or dominant world religion is not only inhumane but also doomed to failure. Religious pluralism is the optimal way to create and sustain a society that is hospitable to the stranger and compassionate to all living things. But first we've got to incarnate this noble vision in our own households.

Generational diversity should also be a priority. Expert ecclesiologists point to three ingredients in the makeup of a thriving church: good worship, sufficient money, and remembering the children. Everything else is extra. There is a caveat: to remember the children means not merely to program *for* them, but *with* them. To cherish our little ones means to bring them unconditionally into the membership of the church. It means to companion and be companioned by them.

Naturally, generational diversity covers the full spectrum, from the very youngest to the very oldest in our churches. Too few of our congregations have adequate, let alone vital, programming for sages and crones. Or maybe it's the young adults who are either missing or skipped over in your parish's programming. The challenge is to have religious learning opportunities of substance for all ages, for everyone who might choose to enter our gates.

A Beloved Community needs holy occasions when all ages gather together to worship and play, learn and serve. The healthiest congregations in our movement are those that not only have age-appropriate programming for children, youth, and adults but also regular intergenerational celebrations—a sterling illustration of promoting unity amidst diversity.

The ways in which this is done are multifarious. Each congregation discerns and invents its own forms. But do it we must. For the overall religious education of Unitarian Universalism is neither book- nor guru-centered. It isn't adult or even child-centered. It's congregation-centered, wherein all ages cooperatively engage in what Starr Williams called a "cycle of nurturing." There are few places in town where intergenerational programming is integral to the mission. A church is one of them.

Back in 1975, when we lived in Davenport, Iowa, our church family went roller-skating. It was early evening and the rink was filled mainly with teenagers and younger children. Our son, Rusty, six years old at the time, was just learning to skate. I, with a grand total of four mostly disastrous skating excursions under my feet, was his teacher. I didn't tell Rusty, but back on the West Coast, I still held a rink record for most "unforced" spills in one session.

We were skating when the loudspeaker invited both boys and girls to retreat to opposite sides of the floor. It was time for the snowball skate dance, the "biggie" of the evening. I was the only adult out there at the time, and I loomed large and old amid the crowd of youthful folks. The music cranked up. It was girl's choice. George, Jack, Max, Joshua, Pete and others successively left our male ranks. Then Rusty was asked to skate by an older girl, a move that fit the trend. Tentatively, with a half-smile, he rolled off. Near the end of the song. I was the only remaining male on the ice. I was about to sneak off the floor and drown my sorrows in a Pepsi when one teenage girl said to another, "Okay, okay, I'll take Methuselah!" I looked around to see where the elderly gentleman might be when I felt a hand grasp mine and yank me off into the swirl.

Well, there you have it: Our beloved clans include babies and Methuselahs and all ages in between. May we never forget that for our communal dance to soar—truly soar—we must all be swooped up into it.

Balance Justice and Joy

6

If the world were merely seductive, that would be easy. If it were merely challenging, that would be no problem. But I arise in the morning, torn between a desire to improve (or save) the world, and a desire to enjoy (or savor) the world. This makes it hard to plan the day.

—E. B. White

A ROBUST CONGREGATION urges parishioners to save and to savor the Creation in cadence. Our days without compassion grow hedonistic. Our journey without pleasure turns us grim. The challenge for individual explorers and congregations is to juggle moments of both duty and delight. Sometimes they turn out to be one and the same—as when we celebrate justly and do justice work joyfully. Or as the Zuni people phrase it, "We dance for pleasure and the good of the city."

Is Unitarian Universalism a saving force or a serving faith? Or some of both? In one of his sermons, the Reverend Scott Alexander exhorts our congregations to "help save the human enterprise . . . save it at every level: myself, others, our culture, and the planet." In her poem "A Hard Death," Unitarian Universalist May Sarton feels differently: "We cannot save, be saved, but we can stand before each presence with gentle heart and hand. . . ." Many of us have experienced saving moments in our own lives, and have seen our churches transformed into enlightened—even saving—presences time and again. But most liberal religionists would willingly settle to be a source of service, because even when we cannot save the world, we must certainly serve it.

Unitarian Universalists endorse the conviction of Church of the Larger Fellowship member Albert Schweitzer, "My life—my argument." We contend that love is an activity, not merely a feeling or attitude; and as such, love only exists in action. A Talmudic tale reminds us that when Moses struck the Red Sea with his wand, nothing happened, but that very same Sea opened when somebody plunged in. Only when we dare to risk acting rather than merely thinking or promising something will there be results.

In growing the Beloved Community, one will find copious opportunities to serve, to "take our bodies where the trouble is," to use the animated phrase of civil rights activist James Bevel. The possibilities for living out our sense of social responsibility are manifold, through social education, service, witness, and action. In our congregations, some will gravitate to activism for peace, reproductive choice, or environmental or economic justice. Others will focus on AIDS programs. Still others will give their energies to anti-oppression work. We are freethinking mystics with hands, and as such, we perceive a thousand worthy social causes clamoring for our talents and resources. Each of us must find ways of serving the cosmos that match our gifts, claim our enthusiasm, and permit us "to win some victories for humanity," to use nineteenth-century Unitarian public education advocate Horace Mann's emphatic phrase.

As members of a servant faith, we aspire to pursue self-fulfillment without falling prey to narcissism and to embody compassion without succumbing to sentimental do-goodism. Emerging from the radical wing of the Protestant Reformation, Unitarian Universalists hold ardently to the doctrine of the "priesthood of all believers," which means that every one of us has the final say on our own convictions and judgments. Unitarian Universalist theologian James Luther Adams amended this principle to call us to the *prophethood* of all believers, meaning that every parishioner is beckoned to share a piece of the moral action. That's precisely the metaphor suggested by social action chair Lynn Eldred in her charge to the San Diego Unitarian Universalist congregation:

> We all have a pocketful of puzzle pieces, representing the skills and experiences we contribute to the common good. I can pocket my pieces, hoarding them, or I can play them. If I do a cost-benefit analysis of working for social justice, I might never play these pieces, because it takes a leap of faith to step up to the table of history and say, "I'm willing to commit myself to making changes."
>
> There are no guarantees, and we can't see the cover of the box to know where to place the pieces or how the pattern will come out. To play these pieces means to play with faith, knowing we may never even see the frame constructed in our lifetime. Perhaps some of the puzzle I work on will never be completed. But I need to play my pieces anyway.

We all have pieces to contribute. We can either pocket them or play them, risk failure or miss the chance to help change history. Our lives, as individuals and as institutions, will be immeasurably enriched whenever we risk playing our singular pieces. But there are some cautions for our prophetic congregations to heed on the road toward liberating ministry. First, we need to be focused, but not driven, in our social activism. Unless we feel good—even gratified—about our moral obligations, we will grow resentful and perhaps burn out. Our congregations need to "share in the action and passion of our times under penalty of being judged not to have lived," to use the phrase of Unitarian Supreme Court Justice, Oliver Wendell Holmes, Jr.—but we need to do so with a sense of perspective and delight. Liberal minister Howard Thurman's insight is extremely useful here:

> Do not ask yourself what the world needs. Ask yourself what makes you come alive, and then go and do that. Because what the world needs is people who have come alive.

When we're awake and exuberant in our compassionate work, great things occur. Indeed, serving and savoring are often wed.

We should also wisely practice the art of dispensability. Often our church social outreach efforts reveal more about our own needs than those of the people we're attempting to serve. If we cling to a cause or client even after closure has occurred, then we know that our involvement is likely to be more compulsive than chosen.

Healthy activist parishes are willing to move on, move back, move over:—to move *on* from our pet cause to another more urgent one, to move *back* from someone who once needed us but no longer does, and to move *over* so that someone else can take our place. To negotiate these various movements, whether as an individual social activist or as a congregational task force, requires both maturity and the willingness to admit to our dispensability.

Prophets should also pursue those projects that not only mesh with our desires but also with our capabilities. Healthy churches use their finite resources to focus upon those problems in their own backyard. As Unitarian Universalists, we simply can't be all things to all people. We're a religious minority, and as such, there are many things we can't do, but we can do some things and do them well. A healthy congregation discerns and selects those tasks it can best fulfill at any given time. Activists need to be concerned about results.

A congregation's social outreach also needs to beware of growing more committed to breadth than depth. Our recurrent weakness is promoting too many resolutions, with too few facts undergirding them, too little time to debate the pros and cons, and too few teeth in our pronouncements once we've endorsed them. The result: too little notice! But, in recent times, with our Association's commitment to "ethics in action," we've been melding spirituality with activism (what the Buddhists call "engaged spirituality"), and our servanthood has grown more holistic and realistic.

Additionally, we dare not forget that prophets, even the finest of the lot, are imperfect creatures who go through periodic bursts of moral flabbiness or fanaticism. To complicate matters, prophets are not always appreciated, within or beyond their walls. So, beware of signing up, as an individual, a task force, or an entire congregation, to do social action in order to gain friends and influence people.

And remember, social justice outreach can't be sustained without oodles of humor and incessant merrymaking. Consequently, healthy congregations are summoned to savor as well as to serve the universe. The medieval poet Kabir penned: "Suppose you scrub your ethical skin until it shines, but inside there is no music, then what?" And, on the other hand, suppose your soul is flooded with song, but the music never gives birth to acts of mercy and justice? Either way, our lives and the lives of all those whom we touch, or could touch, are impoverished.

A vital church is the crucible for forging celebratory compassion, mystical activism, soulful service. As anti-racist leader Barbara Majors voiced it during a recent General Assembly,

> Remember that something like racism that has been mantled can be dis-mantled. However, becoming an anti-racist faith will not be easy. But if it ain't easy, it might as well be fun.

Authentic community-weavers of the sacred web take their mission seriously but never grimly—recalling that the German word for blessedness, *seelisch*, is directly related to *silliness* in English. As the poet Edward Field reflected, "If someone is to lead us, let it be a small person who doesn't ask us to follow but just goes for their own heart's sake, someone who talks a little silly sometimes." Did you know that those in Martin Luther King's inner circle often remarked how comical and zany he could be? This giant moral visionary was also a prankster.

The reasons for creating wholly joy in our beloved communities are manifold. First, joy helps makes us flexible. Taoism observes that in a storm it's the bamboo, the flexible tree, that can bend with the wind and survive. The rigid tree resists and falls victim to its own insistence on control. Sound familiar? In church

life, flexibility is critical to sustaining a shared ministry of servanthood. And how do we stay flexible? By swaying in dance and
song, by leaping to the bounce of life's drumbeat, and, frankly, by
scheduling a regular array of parties on church campus. And, yes,
meditation groups and yoga classes help too.

Merrymaking grants us perspective and resilience when we're
embroiled in serious, taxing church work. Henry Ward Beecher
offered, "Someone without a sense of humor is like a wagon without springs; they're jolted by every pebble in the road." Stern crusaders have little, if any, built-in shock absorption. Enjoyment
delivers fuel to our deliberations and actions, keeps them lubri-
cated, on course. Every protest movement in human history has
been powered by songs of resistance and by playfulness.

Often in social justice work we become burdened and beaten
down. Feeling inadequate in the face of the odds, our clear thinking stops and we hanker for a fresh outlook. We need to bear in
mind that we're called to be faithful, not successful; and that what
we're doing is right. Our spirits can be buoyed by a bracing dose
of affection, the accepting embrace or uplifting tune of a com-
rade. Campaigners for social justice, graced with a sense of mirth,
refuse to travel unaccompanied—otherwise, they may begin to
believe the things the world says about prophets. In short, joyful
crusaders know that they can place both their consciences and
dancing shoes alongside those of their buddies in the bosom of
the Beloved Community.

Healthy congregations also remember that merriment leads
to productive social outreach. Unitarian Universalism encourages
a tempered, not naïve, cheerfulness. We are not doomsayers,
prophesying that Armageddon is coming; nor do we spout blind
optimism, asserting that things will work out fine if we will only
think positive or massage crystals.

Rather, our religion contends that there's sufficient reason for
hope in a good outcome to motivate us to act for change. Why?
Because Earth is a fertile, supportive place and because we
humans are recovering, however slowly, from the erroneous

notion that we're separate from and above all other life. However, the world in the twenty-first century will be more crowded, more polluted, less economically and ecologically stable, and more vulnerable to violent disruption. Life for billions will be more precarious later in the twenty-first century than it is now.

There is a midrash that says that when God created Adam, God escorted him around the Garden of Eden and showed him all the trees, then said, "Do you see my handiwork, how beautiful it is? Be careful not to ruin and destroy my world, for if you do, there will be no one after you to repair it." This command is still applicable—even more so today. We moderns must not despair in the face of the challenge, nor give up when we fall short, but instead we must live up to our great potential for serving and savoring as co-partners with Divine Mystery.

To summarize, serving-and-savoring congregations gaze at reality with eyes of compassion: embracing the stranger, even loving the heart of the enemy, while still possessing the courage to protect the powerless and innocent—and maintaining a sense of hilarity and verve through it all. Theodore Parker, one of our premier workhorses for justice, who harbored fugitive slaves in his home, noted with alarm the glaring absence of any exuberance among his mid-nineteenth-century Unitarian colleagues: "Most powerfully preaching to the conscience and the will, the cry was ever 'duty, duty! work, work!' They failed to address with equal power the spirit, and did not also shout 'joy, joy! delight, delight!'"

So, our congregations of revolutionary justice-makers will be smart to include an abundance of jesting, singing, frolicking, and dancing. We march relentlessly forward, rolling back assumptions and resisting prejudices, while ushering in greater approximations of justice and joy.

Often in justice work we are overwhelmed, a pall descends, our clear thinking stops, and we need a bracing dose of affection from our cohorts as well as plenty of light touches. I remember the end of a brilliant concert when composer-singer Holly Near said sometimes she started feeling grim about torture, racism, nuclear power, and sexism. Her brother pulled her aside, smiled at Holly, gave her a hug, and said buoyantly, "Yeah, so what else do you want to do with your life, Holly?"

Indeed, what else could we have, choose, or want to do with our lives as Unitarian Universalist congregations than to be hopeful, lifelong carriers of justice and joy?

Look Back, Around, and Ahead

I am of the opinion that my life belongs to the whole community, and as long as I live, it is my privilege to do for it
what I can. I want to be thoroughly used up when I die. Life
is no brief candle for me. It is a sort of a splendid torch
which I have got hold of for a moment, and I want to make
it burn as brightly as possible before handing it on to future
generations.

—George Bernard Shaw

IN PURSUIT OF THE Beloved Community, the past is cherished, the
present is celebrated, and the future is charted. Genuine community doesn't just dwell in the present moment; it's vertical as well
as horizontal, traveling backwards and forwards in time. Robust
congregations pay homage to those spiritual comrades who have
come before and honors those not yet born, remembering that
our mission is to give succeeding generations the precious gift of
tomorrow.

The early Celts believed in "thin places," sacred locations scat-
tered throughout the British Isles where one can experience an
almost gossamer divide between past, present, and future, places
where a pilgrim is somehow able to touch a more ancient reality
within present time. May our Unitarian Universalist congregations be sacred sites marked by our own distinctive symbols, pro-

grams, and spirit—thin places that creatively merge the past, present, and future.

Healthy churches dare to look back, cherishing the past. Lot's wife looked back and became a pillar of salt. This biblical legend symbolizes that a person for whom only memories are left often approaches an inorganic state, becomes like stone. Even when our future looks bleak and our present feels blah, we become museum pieces if we focus only on the past.

But if we fittingly salute the agonies and ecstasies of yesterday as well, then it's entirely possible to look back without becoming a pillar of salt. And the best place to negotiate this historical swirl is within the bosom of a sacred fellowship. The church remains one of the few pan-generational communities around. It's a place where children, youth, and adults interact; and it's a site with a history, however short, that travels backward and stretches ahead. The church, as a living community of memory and hope, can rightly be called humanity's memory-keeper.

The word *tradition* literally refers to something valuable being passed into our hands for us to hold with care and mold with diligence for the duration of our trusteeship, and then to release, with much faith, into the hands of successors whom we may not know. While Unitarian Universalists are not ordinarily characterized as traditionalists, our churches are surely the stewards of an immensely venerable "living tradition" from which we constantly draw inspiration and nourishment.

A vital church ensures that all children, youth, and adults—everyone in its communal circle—become familiar with the illustrious, often marginalized history of Unitarian Universalism and with the chronicle of their particular religious outpost. It's critical for members to read firsthand about our chosen spiritual ancestors, to know who they were and what they treasured, even as we assume the mantle of history-makers here and now.

An African sentiment declares that the dead both comfort and prod the living in this life. Truly, our ancestors, remain active members of any current religious clan. They've paid for us and must never be forgotten. A lively congregation rummages regularly in its archives. It displays photos of former members. It names rooms after famous Unitarian Universalists. It transmits anecdotes from the past in current newsletters. It buries members on its premises. It respects its elders during their lifetimes and well beyond the grave.

At First Church in San Diego, there is a memorial wall with plaques listing the names of community kin who have died. While giving a tour of our beautiful grounds to visitors, I would point out the buildings and gardens first; then, at the end of the tour, standing in front of our memorial wall, I would comment: "Now I'd like you to meet the rest of the community," and would proceed to recount stories about the deceased. Memory is a sacrament, and we are buoyed by the wisdom that nothing dies that is remembered. In our San Diego parish we saluted the deceased in a simple yet poignant Sunday morning ritual-blessing: "We would extinguish the flaming chalice to mark Susan's physical death, yet the memories of her special character and gifts live on in our lives. Susan's beautiful spirit is indomitable. We now light a candle to symbolize her influence, which endures. In mystery we are born, in mystery we live, and in mystery we die." If we remember and are remembered, life endures, meaning reigns, hope perseveres.

Mature parishes also look around, celebrating the present. While it's important to look back with gratitude and ahead in anticipation, a healthy church expends the bulk of its energy looking around in the present moment. It majors in being awake now, the only real time. It harnesses what Theodore Parker referred to as "the terrific energy of this age." Enlightened congregations don't live only *for* the present but they do live fully *in* the present.

Golfers are often asked, "What's the most crucial shot in golf?" The most useful reply is, "the one I'm about to make." That's eminently true in church life. The most important worship service, action project, budget process, is the one you're engaged in right now. The litmus test for a mature church is, are we fully present and accounted for as a congregation, right where we dwell, in this historic moment?

Churches that live in the present are content communities, yet never satisfied ones. They remain in motion—sometimes commotion—perpetually trying to improve and evolve. They walk the narrow rail between serenity and smugness. They aren't dreaming about yesterday or fantasizing about tomorrow. They travel with the essential resources they have and the gathered people they are.

My mother is ninety-five years old, and one of the secrets to her long and gratifying life is her sense of equanimity—enjoying what she has rather than whining about what she doesn't have. She blesses and is blessed by the time, the energy, the resources, and the connections she possesses, however imperfect and limited. Sound doctrine for our liberal churches as well.

Finally, healthy congregations look ahead, charting the future. The responsibility of a shared ministry is to produce a communal vision that includes yet transcends the disparate viewpoints of members. As one of the Unitarian congregations in England declares, "A vision without a task is but a dream. A task without a vision is drudgery. A vision with a task is the hope of the world." Parishes can sputter along without vision, but not live abundantly, let alone grow into Beloved Communities. A church exists to be a beacon of justice and enlightenment, compassion and open-mindedness for the larger world. Unitarian Universalism is a forward-looking faith. As Ed Schempp said years ago,

> Unitarian Universalism is faith in people, hope for tomorrow's child, confidence in a continuity that spans all time. It looks not to a perfect heaven, but toward a good earth. It is respectful of the past, but not limited to it. It is trust in growing and conspiracy with change. It is spiritual responsibility for a moral tomorrow.

Visionaries are like Leonardo da Vinci, who traveled with a small sketchpad strapped to his belt, observing reality incessantly. They envision the ideal they want to be. They see ahead, keeping their eyes glued to the vision of the Beloved Community. Religious pilgrims need the vision both of eagles, who view the overall landscape from afar, and of mice, who experience details at ground level. Mature churches harbor hunches about where beauty and justice lie, and more importantly, have the courage to trek there—coaxing, even goading, others to join the caravan.

Every congregation will shape its peculiar eschatology, or vision statement, in alignment not only with our Unitarian Universalist Principles but also in response to its actual location and moment in history. But what we all hold in common is the obstinate conviction that human beings are essential, not tangential, contributors to the stream of history. Making that fundamental claim inspires liberal religionists to make of this universe a lovelier and more just place for all life, starting with our own bodies, radiating forth to embrace our church body, then extending outward to nurture the cosmic body.

The crucial psychospiritual energy for charting our communal future is hope, "a commodity our churches should have in abundance," as Unitarian Universalist minister George Marshall wrote. Indeed, the real division between healthy and ailing congregations is between the energetic, the buoyant, and the hopeful on the one hand, and the enervated, the cynical, and those who are devoid of vision on the other.

Hopers are activated human beings who arouse in self and others a passion for the possible. Hope is the sense of possibility in the midst of, not in spite of, trouble and tumult. Hopers are realists, harboring no illusions about the arduousness of growing the Beloved Community.

Augustine insightfully remarked, "Hope has two beautiful daughters. Their names are anger and courage: anger at the way things are and courage to see that they don't remain the way they are." Our churches are called to become places where such a dynamic conception of hope thrives.

Recently, we received a letter that illustrates the substance of hopefulness, our human capacity to keep reforming, all our days and nights. It came from a man who was offering an apology, as well as making amends, in order to get on with his life. Twenty-five years ago, before our tenure as ministers, a twelve-year-old boy had attended a worship service at the First Unitarian Universalist Congregation of San Diego, after which he stole a microphone lying on the pulpit. He stole it because he hankered to stand in front of his mirror at home and pretend to be a rock star. A typical youthful fantasy. But as he put it in his letter, "This deed has continued to haunt my consciousness. And now at the age of thirty-seven, with four children, I'm determined to be a better father, husband, and person. I'm trying to live my life in a more positive, spiritual manner. The guilt and shame that I feel about what I did is interfering with my ideal. What I did was wrong and I'd like to repay the Church now." He sent us a sizable check that we immediately deposited in the Sound Committee coffers, earmarked for future microphone needs.

We all have similar church stories of sin and repentance, hurt and hope, which tell us that human dignity ultimately lies not in our innocence or goodness so much as in the mettle to forge new beginnings—in bona fide struggles, born of anger and courage. Seven times down, eight times up—making comebacks, falling forward. That's what hope is all about. And it is a basic nutrient of strong congregations that eagerly cherish the past, celebrate the present, and chart the future.

Spread Our 8 Good News

Just do it! Start talking every day to someone about something that happens in your church. By doing it, you'll get better at it. The Unitarian Universalist community will be enriched and made stronger by your being a witness for our faith.

—Sue Turner

WITHOUT GETTING CRANKY or precious, there are times when we have to set the record straight about Unitarian Universalism. We're an historically viable and theologically genuine alternative. We have to internalize that truth and then spread the message.

In her novel *Fly Away Home*, American poet and novelist Marge Piercy has a mother say of her daughters, "The girls had been raised Unitarian Universalist, which seemed a nice, sensible compromise between having no religion at all and having to lie about what we believe. Enough religion to be respectable, but not enough to get in the way."

That lampoon rings true for too many Unitarian Universalist congregations across the land. But we can do better than that, can't we? Because, at heart, we're a faith that truly does get in the way (our own way as well as that of society) and induces us to live not inoffensive, but deeply compassionate, occasionally abrasive, lives. We'll never be a conventionally respectable religion, but we can claim to major in respect toward all living creatures. We're a sturdy, substantive religion, and once we believe in our empowering relevance, we'll project our faith more forthrightly and unashamedly out into the larger world.

Since ours is an unknown or mystifying religion to so many (in our own ranks, not to mention outsiders), we have to become far more conscious about communicating our faith. We need to locate the enduring essence of who we are, then become infectious promoters of our peculiar brand of good news. How many of our aunts or brothers, neighbors or work associates could benefit from a crisper, clearer summary of Unitarian Universalism? And how about the average person walking the streets of this land? Not all these folks will end up agreeing with our message, but our mission is accomplished if they simply comprehend us better. For while being agreed with is not a fundamental human need, being understood is.

Healthy parishes motivate members to claim, clarify, and communicate our liberal religious gospel along the byways of our lives. Here's a short primer course on who we are and who we might become. As Unitarians, we hold that every living creature is inherently valuable and is to be treated as such. We also contend that the cosmos is unitary, that reality is indivisible and whole, that God/Goddess, the Infinite Spirit, is one. As Universalists, we allege that wisdom is discoverable in every era and corner of the universe; that the only salvation worth having is communal, not individual, and that all creatures are held in the eternal embrace of a loving deity.

Unitarian Universalism, then, is our historical identity and institutional allegiance, the crew with whom, for better and for worse, we've hitched our souls. We're not a fly-by-night operation. Our tale goes back four and a half centuries and more.

Our assignment is to tell friends of the heart or strangers on the road not only what Unitarian Universalism means in general but also how it has challenged or comforted us on our particular sojourns. We need to boldly talk about the ways in which liberal religion influences our work life, our ethical commitments, and our family bonds.

Unitarian Universalism is a confessional faith. We are confessional in that each of us is ultimately accountable for stating, then living, our own bedrock convictions. The individual is profoundly prized in our midst. Few of us inherited this grand faith; most of us chose it. So, while we don't pretend to be a chosen people, we are a choosing people.

Therefore, if someone asks what our Church believes, we can kindly respond, "Well, congregations don't actually believe; individual members do. So, if you're interested, let me share some of the principles and values to which I give my loyalty—daily. Then I'd gladly learn of yours!"

Some people, upon hearing that we are a confessional rather than a creedal faith, assume we're something bizarre or illegitimate, perhaps a cult. But consider the true definition of cult—"an extremist religion living outside the society under the direction of a charismatic leader." The Davidians in Waco, Texas, yes—but not Unitarian Universalists. Ours doesn't resemble the mindset of a cult in any way, shape, or fashion. As Unitarian Universalist minister Susan Milnor testifies,

> There has been nothing extremist in our long history of promoting tolerance and equality in the major social and moral issues of this world. There was nothing extremist in our commitment to help free the people of Europe from the savagery of Hitler. There is nothing extremist in our promotion of the spiritual search within a responsibly free religion.

Describe what a cult is; then explain who we are, historically, philosophically, and ecclesiastically.

Unitarian Universalists are protesters. Our congregations are historically rooted in the radical wing of the sixteenth-century Protestant Reformation. Bona fide protesters resist injustice and counter falsehoods as well as *pro-testare*—"testify on behalf of"— all we hold dear. Hence, our faith heritage majors in affirmation and minors in denunciation. In truth, you might say Unitarian Universalists are small-p protestants as well as small-c catholics—the latter in the sense of being comprehensive in scope and holistic in our approach to matters religious.

Unitarian Universalists are called to converse, not to convert. "Speaking the truth in love" (a phrase from the Christian scriptures) is the litmus test of wholesome dialogue. Truth without love turns callous, even cruel. Love without truth is sentimental, even vacuous. So a healthy church charges its members to speak their faith with passion and without fear or equivocation but with caring regard for the humanity of the person across the table. We should always convey our religious heritage and identity as if speaking to someone we respect and value. So, whenever and wherever we are beckoned to communicate our faith, let us remember to wear our principles lightly—seriously, but never grimly. May we share our beautiful faith with a smile—not a saccharine one, but a sincere, luminous one.

Unitarian Universalism is a complicatedly simple religion. Clarity, not obfuscation, is the goal of sound evangelism in a robust congregation. Being opaque or abstruse is inexcusable. Unitarian ancestor and Supreme Court Justice Oliver Wendell Holmes said, "I would not give a fig for the simplicity this side of complexity, but I would give my life for the simplicity on the other side of complexity."

No matter how profound, poetic, or passionate our Unitarian Universalist claims might prove, they remain signposts not hitching posts, inadequate words signaling universal truths shrouded in mystery. We concur that "the Tao that can be written or spoken is not the real Tao." We finally surrender to the wondrous mystery of existence rather than trying to solve it.

Unitarian Universalists articulate our faith contextually. Different occasions dictate varied modes of sharing. A sermon is not the same as a letter. A bedtime talk with your own child contrasts markedly with engaging a stranger at the market or comforting a grieving friend in the hospital. Context matters.

Aspire to be succinct yet ready to amplify. Most crucially, one's gospel is nestled deep in the soul rather than printed in any brochure and hungers to be shared existentially and imaginatively. People are more inspired by shining anecdotes or visceral stories than by tedious explanations. So spend time being a Unitarian Universalist next to your neighbor rather than defining Unitarian Universalism for them. The medium is the message, and each of us remains a principal medium for Unitarian Universalism, whether at home or at play, at worship or in society.

And by the way, a host of disciplines can be helpful in shaping one's own rendition of our communal faith. Read materials with which you disagree, make notes in your journal, meditate, and speak your truths out loud while alone. And of course, there is great merit in having kinship circles or covenant groups in your church to help you locate, then refine your gospel.

Unitarian Universalists testify with minds on fire. As Emerson put it in his Harvard Divinity School Address in 1838, "The true preacher can be known by this, that he deals out to the people his life—life passed through the fire of thought." Such is the task of all Unitarian Universalist witness, whether from pulpit or pew— to braid heart and mind in daring expression.

One's *credo* is a personal witness to the core of one's spiritual journey. It means more than "I believe, I assert, I contend." It's not equivalent to a philosophical discourse or a social rant. *Credo* literally means, "I give my heart and loyalty to . . . ." Astute credos marry the gifts of both intellect and spirit. The sharing of credos— a five minute (roughly three pages, double-spaced) statement of one's current faith—can be the highlight of weekly worship. Credos spur presenters to select highlights from their religious odyssey, highlighting those affirmations that sustain them during the happy and hard days and nights of life. Sunday morning is the best opportunity for formal credo-sharing, because worship is prime time for the Beloved Community—when we convene to pay homage to the highest and dearest we profess as Unitarian Universalists in the bosom of the gathered congregation.

However, a vibrant shared ministry occasions other contexts when parishioners are emboldened to speak with minds on fire about what binds them together, be it a soulful check-in before the board meeting or during a support group, in an adult religious education class, or prior to launching a social action project. Vital parishes find regular excuses for encouraging members to testify with minds on fire.

Unitarian Universalism has a humble yet proud heritage. Growing churches exhibit neither arrogance nor false modesty but rather sincere humility and robust pride. Assuming a humble posture places our religious quest in proper perspective—rooting us in the soil (humus), keeping us compassionate (humane), and tickling us to laughter (humor).

We are called to bask in genuine self-esteem, knowing that we are a proud and worthy religious tradition, however unorthodox. We're not a marginal movement, however small. People may not have previously heard about Unitarian Universalism, but after they've met you, they will have encountered a spirited representative.

The key to radical growth in our congregations is sufficient numbers of us standing tall and shouting from the housetops, "Hey, look at what I've found at All Souls Church! Come and see with your own eyes and hear with your own ears!" It's crucial that liberal religionists dare to become low-key evangelists. Consider the following question: "If you were on trial for being Unitarian Universalist, would there be enough evidence to convict you?" May our individual and communal answers be, "Yes, and the evidence is mounting!"

Unitarian Universalists are bearers of good news. Pilgrims in the fourth and fifth centuries would travel to remote hermitages of the desert fathers and open a ritual exchange with the sentence, "Give me a word, that I may live!" When people come to our doors, do they find good tidings and liberating words? *Evangel* literally means "good news," and Unitarian Universalism constitutes a hopeful, though relentlessly realistic, message—upbeat news about human nature and life's possibilities. Our shining light needs to emerge from underneath the proverbial bushel. The world hankers for our life-affirming vision, rather than one beset with fear or judgment. After all, we belong to the heritage of Isaiah who wrote,

> God has anointed me to bring good tidings to the afflicted; he has sent me to bind up the brokenhearted, to proclaim liberty to the captives, and the opening of the prison to those who are bound, and to comfort all who mourn. . . . (61:1-2)

Rebecca Parker, president of Starr King School for the Ministry, relates the following story. Mortimer Arias, a Methodist bishop in Bolivia, was visiting a congregation in an extremely poor part of the city, where people were starving. On Sunday morning, he presided at the communion table. The congregation was singing a joyful hymn. The table was spread with an embroidered cloth, and on it stood a chalice and a loaf of bread. Just as the hymn was ending, a small boy slipped through the open doors at the back of the church—a child of the streets, dirty and thin. He raced up the center aisle to the communion table, grabbed the sacramental bread and began to eat it.

"Hey, what are you doing?" the Bishop cried.

The child stopped eating, looked at the Bishop, and said with a face full of utter joy, "They told me there was bread in the church!"

And a little one shall lead us toward our mission. The hurting of humanity always forces the issue, doesn't it? So, here's a telling question: Are our churches offering our Unitarian Universalist version of spiritual and material nourishment to the young and old alike who are hungering and happen upon us? Does our liberal religion village dole out useless stones or nutritious bread?

Unitarian Universalists are ever-evolving. We conclude that we will be measured not only by our achievements but by our aspirations. So we keep stretching our souls, noting that we are members of a Beloved Community in the making. Integrity, not perfection, is the goal in our communication. We may reach plateaus of confidence, but if wakeful, we will seldom rest secure. The faith path leads ahead, all the way to our graves. And perhaps beyond.

A catchphrase of the Radical Reformation was "*Ecclesia reformata, quia semper reformanda est*," meaning, "The church reformed, because it is ever in need of being reformed." This signals that reformation is not usually some process our religious body initiates on its own but rather a creative challenge or push coming from the outside. It's humbling to note that the bulk of major changes our parishes make are impelled more from beyond than launched from within.

In sum, healthy churches, at their fullest, are nudged in rhythmic measure by the Eternal One, external circumstances, and internal drive. I offer a closing legend on spreading our Unitarian Universalist gospel. It tells of a contest between the elephant and the thrush. The elephant boasted that she could make herself heard the farther, and invited the thrush to accept the challenge. The thrush did. Then the elephant raised her trunk and sent forth a piercing blast. The thrush quietly sang its song. The judges went forth to find out how far each contestant had been heard. On and on they went until no one could hear the elephant's sound any longer. Yet, they could still hear ever so softly the song of the thrush. "How could the thrush's song carry farther than the elephant's cry?" asked the judges.

Softly the little bird explained, "The thrush family has sentinels throughout the forest; and when one sings, another takes up the song, and then another and another. So they pass it along until it's carried throughout the land."

Our Unitarian Universalist societies are families of thrushes. Each member must serve a stint as a sentinel so that our individual and communal songs of good news might resound, far and wide, throughout the universe.

Practice 9 Respect

> Justice between people is perhaps the most important connection people can have . . . I now begin to realize the difference in my own life between 'acting in one's self-interest' and 'acting in the interest of one's own best self.'
>
> —John Stoltenberg

IF WE FAIL TO BE practitioners of right relations in our chosen tribes, then our admirable pronouncements and contributions in the larger society are bogus. In actuality, it may be far tougher to practice our Unitarian Universalist Principle of "justice, equity, and compassion in human relations" in our families and congregations than anywhere else.

In the Hebrew scriptures, Nathan must have been terrified to blow the whistle on King David, who had caused the death of Uriah so that he could wed Uriah's wife. But Nathan appealed to David's basic goodness by posing a moral question that nudged David to repentance. As we can see, prophets—the brave ones— dare to confront fraud, incompetence, bigotry, relational abuse, and other life problems, not only in the larger world, but more significantly, in their own backyards.

I remember a colleague fervently goading her congregation to become change agents. When she continued to press the issue, some congregants were perturbed and rose up saying: "Reverend

Joan, we agree with your prophetic message, but we didn't expect you to target us. Why, we thought you were going to give hell to the folks 'out there' not to us 'in here'!"

The number of futile squabbles in our congregations, between religious professionals and laity and among lay members, is astonishingly high. We must do better by and with one another as collaborators in strengthening our Beloved Communities. We desperately need to learn how to argue more constructively as Unitarian Universalists.

During my seminary days, there was nary a word on the ticklish topic of church fights. Today there are plentiful volumes, both incisive and broad, on how to use conflict to best advantage. All Souls Unitarian Church in Colorado Springs, Colorado, has generated a "Covenant of Beloved Community," replete with a collective vision and an agreed-upon code of conduct for co-creating a healthy fellowship., The church has also instituted a thoughtful process for reconciliation, healing, and resolution for those times when its mutually shaped norms are violated. This parish also has a Beloved Community team that helps keeps congregational behavior on course and ensures that every newcomer recognizes, right off the bat, that,

> All Souls is a safe haven that nurtures and enhances personal and spiritual growth. We are a welcoming place where those in our community respect themselves and others. We are a shelter of many beliefs where minority and opposing views are accepted and respected. . . . Being a member of Beloved Community requires learning and practice. . . .

And, we should add, forgiveness.

How can Unitarian Universalist parishes foster right relationships? First, they need to learn how to embrace conflict as inevitable, even desirable. Every viable organization—and a church is no exception—both yearns for stability and pushes for achievement. Harmony is in constant tension with adaptation to new circumstances. Progress is both expansive and disruptive:

progress spells change, change causes anxiety, and anxiety precip-
itates conflict. But conflict is not only unavoidable, it's beneficial.
Hearty turmoil elicits new ideas and understandings. It's the fire
in which a vibrant parish is tempered. As one person said to an
adversary in a church fight, "Thank you for being such a pain.
You've come to me as teacher."

A lack of visible conflict cannot be taken to indicate that congregational life is stable or free from disruptive strains. Indeed, in a
church whose organizational structure is tenuous, members may
well avoid conflict, fearing that it might endanger the group's continued existence. So congregants walk on eggs. They sweep contro-
versies under the rug or store them in the closets, if there's room.

Ironically, genuine conflict frequently emerges in eras of
strength, when a community is swelling in size or morale and is
strong enough to tackle the problem. A healthy church learns to
integrate the forces of stability with the forces of change. It can
bicker gainfully. Opposing opinions can actually create a golden
opportunity—that is, for a church equipped with goodwill and
seasoned turning conflict into growth.

Some congregations are bedeviled by passive-aggressive
behavior, where folks never squarely address their conspicuous
differences; or by constant warfare, where interludes of peace are
rare. But on the whole, most of our liberal religious outposts dwell
someplace in between, where people are sometimes difficult and
conflicts are real and persistent but possible to face.

Healthy churches lift up the pain, create covenantal guide-
lines, and point fellow members in the direction of managing
conflicts, if not resolving them. They learn how to fight fairly, not
cruelly; for impact, not injury.

Healthy churches heed what Native American activist
Catherine Attla calls "the big law of respect." A respectful church
is one where boundaries are kept, saboteurs are confronted, crises
are faced. Good behavior is expected and rewarded. Parishioners
are urged, from the moment they sign the membership book, to
engage one another with an active gaze and a level glance. No, it

reaches even farther back than that: Respect must be evident in the details of church organization and programming from the moment a newcomer crosses the threshold. In a healthy church, members are always asking, What does it mean to practice a kinder regard—whether we are engaged in religious education or social outreach, maintenance or leadership development, liturgy or fund-raising?

To be respectful literally means "to look at something or someone again." The Buddhists call this process "seeing with unfurnished eyes"—that is, eyes empty of mental clutter and inherited furniture. Respectful persons are those who look again at what is readily ignored or missed. They review outworn, debilitating church patterns and consider developing new institutional habits. They stand firm against any conduct that will subvert the Beloved Community. They produce safe-congregation policies to protect children, youth, and adults from abusive behaviors. And perhaps most critically, they look again at their own motives before casting judgment on other folks in the congregation.

Indeed, what would it take to for us to see the holy or the divine in each person with whom we tussle in congregational life? The Hindu salutation *namaste* roughly translates as "I honor that which is sacred in you, or that place where you and I are one!" Practice saying that to yourself as you greet, engage, and tangle with the folks in your faith community. For a day, a week, for always.

Still another way of fostering right relationships in our churches is to risk compromising. Religious peacemaker Thich Nhat Hanh suggests inhabiting a state of "nonstubbornness," where we abandon our set agenda in order to entertain opposing viewpoints. Unquestionably, the most difficult thing in up close relationships, like partnership, family, or church, is to relinquish our sense of being correct, being in control, being the "good guy/gal" in fair or foul weather. The prize of Beloved Community requires placing shared satisfaction over hanging onto one's sense of personal virtuousness. Backbone and tenacity are certainly virtues, but they wreak havoc in a parish when plaited with an air

of haughtiness or rigidity. You can sense a nasty stalemate loom-
ing whenever *we* supposedly hold principles, while *others* merely
harbor prejudices.

Right relations in church life bank on individuals who are willing to resolve conflicts through compromise, not through bully-
ing—or even convincing another of the rightness of our position.
Creative compromises don't always mean giving in to the other
side, but they do mean giving up being right all the time. Each person promises to contribute something for the benefit of the greater
institution, instead of bolstering her/his own opinion or ego.

Compromise clearly activates our imagination, and often our
deepest and most compassionate instincts. Journalist Barbara
Walters pointedly asked Anwar Sadat years back, "What would it
take for you to go to Jerusalem to meet with Menachem Begin?"
Suddenly Sadat was examining the obstacles to this goal in a new
way. Imagination reminds us that something else besides stalemate or violence is possible.

Compromise is the hallmark of the human species and a critical factor in our congregational ability to evolve. Only fifteen
percent of our brain is grown before birth. Eighty-five percent
develops afterwards, so we're far more adaptable than we may
have imagined. As one analyst noted about the grand achievements of Eleanor Roosevelt, "She mastered the art of compromising up!" Church stewardship is committed to doing just that.

Finally, congregants should hold themselves to what radical
monk Thomas Merton called "the vow of stability." Individual
Unitarian Universalists may be devoted to a particular viewpoint
in any given church conflict. We should be. Church life should
encourage passionate rather than lukewarm stakeholders. But
allegiance to the common values that establish our church's very
being in the first place must always supersede our own personal
positions. Our early Universalist forebrother Hosea Ballou
echoed the kind of respect that transcends self or personal outlook when he wrote in *A Treatise on Atonement* in 1805, "Let
neighborly love continue. If we have love, no disagreement can

do us any harm, but if we have not love, no agreement can do us any good!"

Every concerned church member has a responsibility to participate in family squabbles rather than duck and seek cover. To remain neutral in times of conflict is to cop out. Not to decide is to decide. Moral philosopher John Dewey put the problem vividly: "Saints deliberate while burly sinners run the world." So church stakeholders must vow to enter the debating chambers, share their piece, listen to their tablemates, then stay put.

One recalls the Last Supper scene with Jesus and the twelve disciples. Jesus breaks bread, passes a cup and says, "Someone here will betray me." That's a pretty painful subject to risk at such a time of fellowship, and Jesus was in fact betrayed by both Peter and Judas before the next day was over. Nonetheless, Jesus didn't flee the scene. He took a deep seat. A healthy church urges us to stay at the table, even when our first impulse may be to disappear as quickly as possible amidst the flying fur.

A vital parish candidly warns its constituents, "Yes, you will be frustrated here sometimes, bruised, perhaps even betrayed upon occasion. And how could it be otherwise? A church, at its truest, isn't a sweetheart festival; and congregants aren't a bunch of unblemished angels but a batch of flawed earthlings. We do ugly things to one another outside the church. Why should we expect to receive perfect treatment inside these walls?"

Granted, there may be times when we feel compelled by conscience to leave our church over a serious issue. If, according to our deepest convictions, our chosen clan has broken faith with its very soul, we may be driven to say, "Bless you and good-bye. Thank you for all you have given me, but I must move on. I can no longer sincerely and affectionately pursue my religious path in your midst." But such a departure should be a last resort.

The Navajo have a practice that illustrates staying at the table during times of glaring distress. When someone has violated a principle or person, the townsfolk gather to burn the offender's home down. Then—and here's the restorative twist—they regroup, and alongside the violator, help to rebuild her or him a new one. If our churches seek to create safe/saving spaces for people who have wounded and been wounded, then it's both intelligent and courageous to take both symbolic and tangible action in cooperation with each other. It could entail role-playing, rearranging furniture, creating a wildly fresh plan, taking a walk, engaging in social protest, praying, planting trees, or even rebuilding a home.

10
Nurture Stewards

They happen in churches
when you're lucky;
other places too, though I mostly
only know ecclesiastical varieties.
Long haul people
upon whose shoulders
(and pocketbooks and casseroles
and daylight/nighttime hours)
a church is built and—
more important—maintained
after the brass is tarnished and
cushions need restitching . . .

For long haul people bless a church
with a very special blessing.

—Rudy Nemser

FULL-SERVICE STEWARDSHIP responsibly attends to self, church, society, and planet—the entire sweep of what the Beloved Community encircles. Robust stewards are summoned to think, then act, both globally and locally. They take regular care of their bodies—what I call "temple maintenance." They affirm the natural universe as their home, revering its gifts, both known and unknown, and committing to just and compassionate husbandry of its resources. But for purposes of this volume, we will focus on stewardship of our churches and those persons whom Unitarian Universalist minister Rudy Nemser affectionately calls "long haul people." *Stewards* are literally "keepers of the hall," folks who labor to keep their chosen religious community spiritually, financially, and programmatically afloat—even lively and growing. Stewardship means drawing upon our highest intentions and most generous aspirations. As James 1:17 states, "Every generous act of giving is from above"—coming from our highest selves.

Stewards always remember that their position as stakeholders is temporary. They co-shepherd a parish for a while, while they have it on loan. Stewards are not possessors; they don't own a church any more than they own a piece of land. They are simply the blessed recipients of a singular period in history. Stewards have been assigned a watch. They are entrusted with our Unitarian Universalist legacy in the place where it comes to them, to handle it with exceeding reverence and care, to shape it while allowing it to shape them, and then to keep the gift moving. Stewards keep vows, keep the books, keep resources flowing, and maintain historical records. Stewards are steadfast servants through thick and thin, through personal regrets, even through dislikes and defeats, because their loyalty is never to eras or trends or personalities alone.

When there's a financial bind, stewards are pacesetters with generosity of gift. When a church school class needs a leader, their hands go up. When there's a maintenance problem, they pitch in without being prodded. When there are newcomers to be welcomed, their smiles are evident. When a difficult, even spiteful, clash flares up, they are reliable bridge-builders.

In the introduction to *Healthy People 2000*, Louis W. Sullivan, former U.S. Secretary of Health and Human Services, declares, "Personal accountability, which is to say responsible and enlightened behavior by each and every individual, truly is the key to good health." Likewise, communal responsibility is the key to institutional health and banks on a sturdy cadre of stewards.

A person went to Henry Ward Beecher and said, "Mr. Beecher, I have a good horse to sell. He's a good family horse, works double or alone, is gentle, intelligent, not easily frightened, will stand without hitching and is thoroughly sound and reliable." Mr. Beecher replied, "I can't buy your horse, sir, but I'd like to have it as a member of my church." You can have a congregation full of fearless dreamers, intellectual giants, historical wizards, mystical activists, and keen educators, but without stewards, few church ventures remain hardy. Stewards are the veritable work-horses of parish life.

Over the years, I've asked congregants to list their highest ideals for Unitarian Universalist character development. Love is duly noted as central to our faith, but so is justice, because love turns sentimental unless grounded in fairness. Trust keeps us going in a world soaked in cynicism. And acceptance embraces friends and makes building bridges with foes possible; what's more important than that? Then there's the unsung virtue of serenity, or equanimity, that anchors us amidst life's turbulence. And courage—who would attempt the religious pilgrimage without sufficient bravery? And of course, there are always votes for joy and forgiveness and humility as well.

But there's one virtue without which one has little or no claim to religious living, without which congregations and societies don't sustain the path toward the Beloved Community. And it's often ignored or underrated, not even appearing on congregants' lists until they are reminded of it. That virtue is generosity— openheartedness, the cardinal ability to give lavishly of yourself to others, to the world around you, to the divine communal Spirit in which we live, move, and have our beings.

Generosity undergirds and underwrites all other values. Without generosity, one loves sparingly, if not stingily; without generosity, our acts of justice happen rarely; without generosity, we hoard our precious gifts of time and soul and other resources.

Generosity is the primary virtue that makes possible the stewardship that sustains our healthy congregations. It's the *sine qua non* virtue. A synonym for generosity is magnanimity, which adroitly combines two Latin words for "large soul" (*magna* and *anima*). Unquestionably, the strongest churches in Unitarian Universalism are those that are large-souled across the boards—spiritually, educationally, prophetically, and fiscally. There's a familiar children's affirmation circulating in Unitarian Universalist worship, replete with gestures, that goes right to the guts of our liberal, generous, magnanimous faith: "We are Unitarian Universalists—a people of open minds, loving hearts, and welcoming hands!"

Let's take a deeper look at how generosity or large-souledness is actually displayed in healthy congregations. First, generous congregations find profound joy in giving. A planned giving professional once remarked that the purpose of his vocation is essentially "to help people find the joy in giving." Truly, the purpose of shared ministry is to accompany people in finding, then liberating, gifts for causes of their deepest choosing. A fundamental question to pose to both veterans and newcomers in congregational life is, What gifts are you ready to cultivate, then release, in your chosen community of faith?

Alas, our brand of liberal religion too often remains a generous faith played out cheaply. Stinginess is one of our peskiest and most pernicious sins. Unitarian Universalism ranks as one of the wealthier denominations in earning capacity, but among the more parsimonious with our giving. We proffer the excuse that our members give liberally to social causes outside the church, more so than do members of conservative faiths. This may be the case, but it's an explanation, not an excuse.

Unitarian Universalist minister Jay Deacon tells the story that one day Alexander the Great was triumphantly entering a city that had fallen to his forces, when a beggar dared to approach his entourage and raised a feeble arm toward the conqueror, in the timeless gesture of begging for alms. When Alexander tossed him some gold coins, a courtier asked him why he'd given the beggar gold when all he needed or expected were copper coins, Alexander answered, "Copper coins would have met the beggar's needs; but gold coins meet mine."

When we give liberally of our dearest resources, we're genuinely fulfilled in the process. Truly becoming what we claim to be, namely, a *liberal* religious church, requires us to be generous to the core—open of mind, heart, spirit, and hand. Healthy persons and healthy congregations know and practice the supreme joy of giving. Our personal and communal lives will be weighed at the proverbial judgment day by the size of our generosity. May the epitaph on our tombstone read, "What I gave, I have. What I spent, I had. What I kept, I lost."

Generous congregations are also unremitting in combating our pervasive culture of greed. Our world is geared to acquisition; hence, we frequently hear greedy pitches like, "This is yours for the taking" or "Here's a deal just for you!" Take this, take that, take power, take advantage, take over. There's the story of the child who saw a rainbow for the first time and was startled by its beauty and brilliance. Then she turned to her mother and asked, "What's it advertising?" What a sad commentary on contemporary culture's emphasis on materialism. The number of seductive gimmicks peddling something for nothing or very little is shocking. Our wider society has found it agreeable to allow raffles, bingo games, off-track betting and casino gambling, among other financial shortcuts.

In *The Little Virtues*, essayist Natalia Ginzburg argues that we should teach our children "not the little virtues but the great ones. Not thrift but generosity and an indifference to money; not caution but courage and a contempt for danger; not shrewdness but frankness and a love of truth; not tact but love for one's neighbor and self-denial; not success but a desire to be and to know."

Of course, the minor virtues have their place in life, but the large-souled ones inspire a deeper sense of meaning and purpose and should be taught through our adult example and modeled in the lives of our Beloved Communities. We must give our children more than an obsession with getting something for nothing.

Churches must help society focus on compassion as our human imperative rather than on prosperity as our divine right.

However, modern religion is not exempt from the temptations of greed. The number of enticements offered by spiritual gurus is staggering. A healthy church must counter such bribes by insisting that there are challenges and costs on the religious expedition. There's no such thing as a free lunch, even in our free religion.

A generous church inhabits a giving-receiving continuum. During the offering time, you will likely hear a balanced invitation such as, "Some say it's more blessed to receive than to give, and others claim it's more blessed to give than to receive. What we urge in our liberal religious community is this: When we give, to give generously, with an open hand and heart, and when we receive, to receive gratefully, with an open hand and heart as well."

Why is generosity so critical to the life of the Beloved Community? What are the benefits we reap in the process of being generous folks? First, those who give generously are healthy people. In the words of the eminent psychiatrist, Karl Menninger, "Money giving is a symptom of a person's emotional health. Generous people are seldom mentally ill." No surprise, because church givers don't have energy to waste on being distraught or bitter. They're too busy serving beyond their own aches and egos. They're planting seeds of new life with their gifts. They're healing and helping others through their generosity, and in so doing, keeping hale and hearty themselves.

Magnanimous givers also live longer. Countless studies have demonstrated that people with social bonds—close friendships and religious membership—have lower mortality rates. So if you join a Unitarian Universalist church, get involved and pledge to make a difference, we can't promise a hunk of celestial property, but it looks like your earthly stay will be lengthier.

Givers also feel proud and empowered. When we're generous, our self-esteem soars. That's why healthy churches encourage members not to give until it hurts but to give until it feels good— to give until it helps, to give until we're carrying our fair share of the financial load. We're beckoned to give until we can say with a clear conscience, "All right, now that's a generous, responsible pledge to my faith community that's been so very good to me!"

In short, some wag noted that in order to write a decent biography of a person, you'd need access to his or her checkbook. Money is a vivid means of placing value on the many goods available in society and is one way of staking out our priorities.

Giving to your Unitarian Universalist church is also a good investment. We regularly suggested that our San Diego congregants imagine all the businesses and social agencies that had come and gone since we our congregation was established in San Diego back in 1873. Hardly a month went by but some new enterprise would start in our very neighborhood and disappear before long. First Church is firmly established, solid as a rock, not going anywhere. You can count on its presence and witness. When we give generously to our chosen faith we're investing in a stable and worthy institution.

Giving also connects us with the larger human family. Generosity extends our horizons beyond our own navels. The wider world needs us. Think of what your community would be like without the socially concerned and spiritually vital presence presence of your local congregation. One of the Baptist ministers in San Diego often said about our Unitarian Universalist tribe, "I don't agree with a lot of what you say and do, but I'm appreciative that you're always supporting causes that no other church in town will touch and welcoming folks no one else wants around."

In closing, let it be known that generous congregations are generative ones. They experience the gratification of seeing wrongs battled, prejudices undercut, griefs lightened, communities upheld. They recognize that, in the end, we possess nothing except what we've shared or given away.

Keep Journeying

In the civil rights movement James Lawson and I used to
speak about making Nashville a Beloved Community, a
community at peace with itself. It is a sense of coming
together to serve the common good. The journey toward the
Beloved Community is a journey of a lifetime . . . I speak a
great deal about the possibility of building one house, one
family. And you cannot build one house or one family or
one community if you're not somehow consumed by the
spirit of love.

—John Lewis

UNITARIAN UNIVERSALISM IS FLUID, unsettled, growing—a
movement. Everything matters, because nothing is carved in
stone. As the Unitarian poet e. e. cummings put it, "we can never
be born enough."

For us evolution isn't just a biological fact but a personal and
institutional one as well. According to our tradition, each step of
the religious journey holds some deepening affirmation, some
correcting discipline, some fresh wonder.

Healthy congregations are pilgrims on a hallowed trek.
Members are saunterers, literally "holy-landers," who treat every
stride and piece of turf as conveyors of holiness. Despite dull
expanses and dry spells, parishioners aspire to be persistent plod-

ders, eyes ever on the next plateau, resisting the temptation to camp out in caves of comfortableness.

There are multiple directions to tread on the road to the Beloved Community—downward into the natural order, backward into historical context, outward to broadcast our good news and to serve society, inward to feed our own souls while shepherding our home flock, and upward in prayerful aspiration and gratitude. But the primary direction of healthiness in church life is forward, toward the prize of the holy commonwealth.

The journey is rugged, leads ever onward, and requires inordinate courage and stamina. John Woolman, an eighteenth-century Quaker, was devastated that some Quakers held slaves. To change that state of affairs, he didn't censure the slaveholders. Instead, he traveled on horseback, visiting each slaveholder individually and sharing his moral concern. It took Woolman some thirty years to persuade all of them. But in the end, not one Quaker owned a slave. Passing laws would probably have brought about faster results but not without pain and lingering bitterness. As servant-leaders and as prophetic parishes, our job is to transform people, not merely to enforce rules, always remembering we won't necessarily be as successful as Woolman. Therefore, we're called to be conscientious, even when we fail.

We dwell in a pop culture where intellectual and spiritual pabulum are dispensed daily and where maps to nirvana are passed out on street corners. But genuine religion has nothing to do with a pain-free route to enlightenment. Pilgrim churches on an exodus know they are on a rugged, lifelong quest, clearly not for the fainthearted. The word *travel* is etymologically related to the word *travail*. "Easy" is not a name for our manner of being religious and doing church.

The journey is not only difficult; it is unending. Unitarian Universalism—historically, theologically, and ecclesiastically—is an unfinished adventure. Everyone who enters our sanctuaries reaches not a stopping place but a way station on the road. We sometimes falter or spin out of control, but a healthy church balances personal growth, spiritual awakening, and social justice in creative alignment. We know that we must keep on journeying toward what the Universalists called "the larger hope." Our true direction as a Beloved Community is ever forward. All are asked to bring their special gifts along for the ride. As a new member's litany exhorts, "We need you—your talents and your resources— as you need ours. We believe that we are both blessed in this evolving covenant of membership."

It is unlikely that our congregations will reach the Promised Land during our lifetimes, but like Moses, we can point—even pave—the way. Martin Luther King Jr. proffered a similar perspective as he addressed the striking sanitation workers in Memphis, the night before he was assassinated. King's exhortation reminds us of the creative tension between "what is" and "what might yet become" in growing the Beloved Community wherever we're planted: ". . . and I've seen the promised land. I may not get there with you, but I want you to know tonight that we as a people will get to the Promised Land." Yet, my friend and colleague, Unitarian Universalist minister Thandeka, counters with her own angle on the subject: "we are the Promised Land every time we create a graceful moment of life with self, others, and the world. The realm of God is here and now."

A healthy, vital church is a *becoming* as well as a *believing* one. Those who resist growth in congregational life, either in spirit or statistics, resist vitality. Resting content with the status quo leads inexorably to decline. For a church to fulfill its mission it must be generative—it must grow. Being healthy means being elastic and evolving. Naturally, liberal outposts take stands, usually individually and sometimes institutionally, but we recognize that they are not absolute. Our religion posits a relentless encounter with an ever-shifting reality. A popular evangelical bumper sticker a while back proclaimed, "I've found it." A corresponding Unitarian Universalist sticker would presumably read, "I found something valuable—for now." We draw our conclusions in pencil, not indelible ink.

In Nigeria, people say of someone who has died, "Their feet are in agreement; in other words, they've ceased moving. For the wise elders know that life is movement and movement begins with the contradiction of the limbs . . . non-contradiction means death."

Meadville Lombard Theological School professor David Bumbaugh reminds us that at the trial of sixteenth-century Transylvanian Unitarian theologian Francis David,

> Many of the nobles supported Francis David, [but] the clergy were split. One Calvinist Hungarian demanded the death penalty; and the Jesuits were eager to see the Unitarian leader condemned. In the end, Francis David was found guilty of innovation and condemned to perpetual imprisonment. He died in the dungeon at Deva, November 15, 1579.

The operative word here is *innovation*, and it presages our religious *modus operandi* in ensuing centuries, both as individual pilgrims and in the way we run our churches. We are part of a dynamic venture, not a static organization. We are anchored to no single moment, no particular guru, no one tradition; but we are linked to countless events, persons, and scriptures.

Alfred North Whitehead described God as the Divine Lover beckoning the world into becoming, as any true lover might with a beloved. That is our progressive religious mindset. In short, our Unitarian Universalist congregations constantly nudge their membership to think of themselves not as human beings but as human becomings.

Know That You Are Not Alone

12

Every nation must learn that all the people of the nations are children of God and must share the wealth of the world. You may say that this is impracticable, far away, and can never be accomplished. But this is the work which Universalists are appointed to do. . . . We are not alone. There is always an unseen power working for righteousness. This Infinite is behind us. The eternal years of God are ours. . . .

Dear Friends, stand by this faith. Work for it and sacrifice for it. There is nothing in all the world so important to you as to be loyal to this faith which has placed before you the loftiest ideals, which has comforted you in sorrow, strengthened you for noble duty, and made the world beautiful for you. . . . One God, one law, one element, and one far-off divine event to which the whole creation moves.

—Olympia Brown

THE HEALTHY CHURCH demands a high-stakes relationship with its parishioners. Ecclesiology asserts that the question "Who am I?" is secondary to its partner query, "*Whose* am I?" There are three interlocking dimensions that make up our way of growing a Beloved Community as religious liberals: believing, becoming, and belonging.

We are not self-sufficient creatures. Our Unitarian Universalist heritage claims that we belong not only to ourselves,
our eras, our societies, and our living tradition but also to the
Creation, the Eternal Spirit, and God. If anyone can keep contemporary religious liberals on course, faithful to our communal
vocation, it would be our foresister Olympia Brown. There's a
bronze tablet at Atwood Hall in Canton, New York, commemo-
rating the achievements of this pioneering feminist:

> Olympia Brown was the first woman to be graduated by the
> theological school and St. Lawrence University. Her Univer-
> salist ordination in 1863 made her the first woman in our
> country to achieve full ministerial standing recognized by a
> denomination . . . 'The Flame of Her Spirit Still Burns Today.'

Brown was a tireless campaigner for spiritual fulfillment and
social justice for all of her ninety-one years. We humbly follow her
in the stream of our majestic living tradition. Brown achieved in
her era what we must accomplish in ours as partner-builders of
the Beloved Community. Brown was pragmatic yet focused. A
mystical activist, she advanced the "great lesson," her Universalist
gospel, that all souls "are children of God and must share the
wealth of the world." And by wealth, she meant both material and
spiritual abundance.

Olympia Brown beckons us onward, reminding us neither "to
demand immediate results," nor to labor "without counting the
cost." Furthermore, we must realize that transformational work
"can never be accomplished, but this is the work which we are
appointed to do." However, have no fear, Sister Brown exhorts:
"We are not alone. This Infinite is behind us." And the Infinite is
before, alongside, and ahead of us as well.

So give your all, personally and communally, to that enterprise that has done so much for you. Commit your whole being
to growing and cultivating pieces of the Beloved Community,
here and now, right where you're planted. Ours is a holy vocation,
worthy of all we are.

Consequently, our local congregations go full bore to establish sites of peacemaking, justice-building, and joy-sharing; and then we gladly surrender whatever outcomes we achieve back into the embrace of an Eternal Love that first breathed us into existence, both as persons and as clans.

Brown forecast that there is truly "one God, one law, one element, and one far-off divine event to which the whole creation moves." Her ringing words signal the fierce and abiding unity of our quest. There are undoubtedly secularists and other religionists in our company of travelers as well, for we belong to a progressive, liberating caravan larger than Unitarian Universalism per se.

Remember also that ours is a pan-generational adventure— some have gone before us, some stand alongside us now, and some will join the convoy after we're dead. But all makers of the Beloved Community are ultimately united on this sacred sojourn.

In some fashion, both historical and mystical, "the whole creation moves," in fits and starts to be sure, onward toward what we can only imagine might be the presence of the Beloved Community. At the close of our ecclesiastical jaunts, we fling our communal efforts far into futures beyond our knowing or shaping. We "rest assured," trusting that what we've done and who we've been will measurably contribute to the growing of the Beloved Community. We clasp the products of our labor gently, both holding what we cherish and willing to release it. We return our contributions into the care of those human and divine spirits that endure beyond our lives.

Further, we are responsible to our local congregations and to the greater society. Yet there is more. We belong to an eternal embrace that brought us into being and will never let us go, whatever we've accomplished, however far we've traveled along the path.

Our faith declares that we are held by the Great Spirit when we can no longer hold ourselves. For we are not the ultimate source, sustainer, or summation of the Beloved Community.

This Infinite is. And we belong to it.

The Faith Tree Grows

THE TWELVE HALLMARKS of healthy congregations listed here don't function independently but interdependently. One way to envision this bedrock interrelatedness is through the metaphor of the cosmic tree. It conveys a vivid paradigm encompassing the entire universe as well as our Unitarian Universalist faith, with its huge canopy of branches above, its unseen but vast system of roots below, and its trunk linking these two complex networks. A tree, like a vital church, has the remarkable ability to grow up, out, and down at the same time.

A thriving congregation has a strong root system. A tree without roots topples easily. The rootstock in every Beloved Community needs to be broad and deep—broad in that our communal tree receives nutrients from the soil of various traditions, deep in that sustenance comes through living out our shared symbols and stories in some profound way.

The trunk represents the inner identity of each religious tribe. All that transpires is processed through the trunk. Therefore, the following questions must regularly be asked: Wherein lies the thickness and sturdiness in our congregation? What is its vision, wherein lies its soul? Can I, as a member, describe the trunk of our ecclesiastical tree to a stranger who greets me on the street?

Winston Churchill was dining out one evening, and after tasting the pudding, he hailed a waiter and exclaimed, "It's okay, but it lacks a theme!" Many of our congregations are weakened by lack of clarity. We are notoriously slow to produce a common mission statement that equally inspires the newcomer and grounds the veteran.

The bark of the tree is the living, finite body of our church. Ralph Waldo Emerson spoke of truth, goodness, and beauty as the holy triumvirate of Unitarian values. Beauty represents the weak cousin of the lot, since one of the oft-ignored arenas in parish life is aesthetics. Vigorous, thriving congregations exude an inner and outer sense of balance, proportion, and comeliness. Taking reasonable care of our external temples is not a luxury but essential. The same goes for the grounds, the property, the body of our chosen tribes. The way we groom and beautify our church plants is an unsung yet critical indicator of our vitality and soundness. Any community that manifests shabbiness is destined not only for physical but also for spiritual deterioration.

The branches of the tree denote our compassion as well as our extension. Behold the branches. Hale and hearty parishes reach out to shelter various fellow creatures—be they animals, strangers, or children. The greater society counts on a healthy Unitarian Universalist outpost willing to go out on a limb. Branching out refers to low-key but explicit evangelism as well, extending our reach to any unchurched who might harbor liberal religious leanings. And branches extend upward as well as outward. Growing churches are never ends in and of themselves. They point to sources of wisdom, power, and nourishment beyond their bailiwicks. They incarnate the holy; they speak of transcendence. Their branches reach skyward in gratitude, awe, humility, and yearning.

Finally, the leaves, the flowers, the fruit of our communal trees bespeak the seasonal shifts of every congregational journey. Maturing individuals and tribes know winter and spring, summer and fall. We blossom, we are lush, we drop leaves, we are barren.

Programs, even in the sturdiest of our liberal religious clans, come and go. Yet the faith tree grows. Members leaf and leave, are born, flourish, and die; religious professionals are all interims; buildings are never finished; our noblest actions are flawed—yet the faith tree grows.